I Can Go Home Again After, Right?

A Canal Diary

Jayne Tebbutt

Copyright © 2017 Jayne Tebbutt

ISBN: 978-0-244-30991-6

PublishNation
www.publishnation.co.uk

Thank you Roly for persuading me to do it, thank you Grumpina for being old enough to be abandoned, and thank you Johnsons for helping me get it print ready.

My partner and I decided to give up work and travel about a bit on a canal boat.

Personally, I think it was an unusual mid-life crisis, but he has assured me it was just a break from the world.

Challenging, as the boat was only 57 foot long and 6 foot wide. . .

And despite being together for 9 years, we have never lived with each other.

This book is an amusing diary of our adventures, if you can use the word adventure for the slow amble round some British canals.

Travelling - Nowhere yet
Date - 21/07/14

Well, we have done 3 days on Billow - that's the name of our boat not some new street drug. It has been tough but we haven't killed each other . . . Yet. Still not sure I can actually do this. 6 months without the luxuries of a washing machine or bath. Yes there's a shower but try as I might I cannot drink wine & read a book in the shower, but sitting canal side with a green tea (it is only 9am) reading and listening to the birds and nothing else, maybe I actually can do this.

I met my first official hippy boater and his friends last night. It was going well and my confidence in my ability to rough it was growing, until they tried to convince me to crap in bags & use the dog poo bins to save emptying the toilet!! No, No I cannot do this boating lark, find me a hotel immediately! I nearly ran sobbing to the closest bricks and mortar to demand refuge.

To be absolutely clear, over the next 6 months Roly and I remained human and well trained. Toilets and bags were used as originally designed and were never once confused with each other!

Travelling - The Wharf Bugbrooke - to -North somewhere!
Date - 24/07/14

And we are off, or we will be if he ever wakes up, I'm raring to go. 5 days aboard & we haven't moved yet!

Yesterday Roly tried to show me how to empty the toilet. If the canal water hadn't been so murky I'd have dived off Billow and swum for home. Before agreeing to this trip I made him

1

promise that the toilet would ALWAYS be his job, absolutely no way am I doing that. Shudder.

I have already lost some clothes to the canal. Yesterday, some drying washing (hand washed with such care and diligence) decided it was all too much and threw itself, hangers and all into the water. So with a hearty cry of 'washing overboard' I went looking for the hooky thing (insert technical name if you know it) that lives on top of the boat, by the time Roly returned from emptying the loo (Still very much his job) the only thing I had managed to retrieve was a tea towel, still, at least I know which side of Billow the big hooky thing is next time my washing feels suicidal. Goodbye t-shirts you served me well.

Travelling - Weedon - to - Onwards
Date - 25/07/14

So a busy morning thus far. I've learnt how to pull away and moor up. I've also created a wave by breaking the speed limit. A bit like learning a new language, you want the swear words first, they are more interesting. Although not sure that speeds slightly faster than walking are going to spike many peoples interest but I live on a boat now, I need to be easily pleased.

I also had to deal with one of the things I was most worried about, (no not Roly breaking wind in such a small space, I am familiar with all the emergency exits) Spiders. Bloody great man eating, weird legged, freaky eyed spiders. I would like to say I was cool, calm and collected when I saw it running up my actual leg and that I confidently said to Roly "please can you brush that away". Yes, I would like to say that . . . However, what happened in reality is slightly (massively) different. As I'm steering, concentrating hard due to an approaching bridge I had to squeeze through, I felt a tickle. . . bloody fly I think. I

2

look down ready to swipe it away only to be faced with the meanest hairiest looking spider who no doubt was carry a knife, probably. All hell breaks loose, I let go of the tiller (steering stick, see I am learning), scream, then very sensibly start jumping up and down kicking my legs about, only because I needed to confuse the vicious thing you understand. Jayne, camera and mobile almost go into the canal. As it was 'almost' instead of 'actually' I think I handled it well.

To recover from the trauma, I had to open and close 7 locks, these perfectly manicured nails and soft office hands had to do 7 locks, unbelievable!

7 locks became 14. I am guessing here but locks don't breed so I think he was being liberal with the truth. 14 locks going up should certainly do something for the bingo wings but I am going to ache tomorrow! By lock 6 my office hands were feeling it, so being the gentleman that he is Roly offered me some gloves. I had to decline though as the older couple we were lock sharing with seemed to manage without and I didn't want to look like a big girl.

When I'd had enough of blistering my hands and breaking my nails I thought I would have a go at maneuvering Billow through the locks. Obviously waited until we were without audience, I didn't need the shame of everyone laughing and pointing at my inadequacies. So after we parted company with our lock sharers who, incidentally made my day when the wife declared "rather you, than me" when the pair heard about our 6 month travel plans. Hallelujah, bloody hoorah. I had become so sick of hearing "you will love it", "you'll never go back" that her words filled me with joy, because yes, yes I may (definitely will) want to go back to my actual house. I like my bath, I like my room to swing a cat, not an actual room purely for cat swinging, you understand just a general roominess throughout. So spurred on by the knowledge that not all canal folk are in some cult you can never escape from, I decided to get our boat through a lock!

I may have done the first one with my eyes closed for some of the time, and oddly my boobs kept getting in the way of the tiller (perhaps panic made them swell to 10 times their normal size) but I did it without sinking her or breaking off too many important bits. By the 3rd my eyes remained open, except of course for standard blinking. My boobs behaved themselves and I didn't even touch the lock sides (with the boat not my boobs). I've earnt a massive wine!

Travelling - Crick - to - Ahead
Date - 26/07/14

Last night was our 7th night onboard and I'll be honest, if there had been a taxi canal side at 2am I'd have climbed in shouted home now and step on it, I would have never looked back. I was too hot to sleep, but too tired not to. The other half says the hot water tank is under the bedroom which will be lovely in the winter. That is as maybe but It's July and I was melting He won't have the portholes open because of mozzi's, I would have rather been eaten to death than boiled to death. I eventually slept on the sofa with all the portholes open, so there! I got a breeze and it was lovely, but the sofa is supposed to be where he sleeps if (when) we have a row, may have to rethink that for summer. Thankfully my sense of adventure returned this morning so full steam ahead.

Aside from the stunning scenery, over friendly ducks and swans, vibrant insects and quirky boats I've seen an awful lot of dead animals floating lazily on the water. 3 rabbits, 1 fox and 2 hedgehogs. Never really thought of it before but once they have fallen in they can't get out, it's not like their friends have the option to throw them a life ring. Think I may start building little animal ladders along our journey.

Incidentally, upon examining myself this morning, not a single bite and yes, of course I enjoyed telling him this fact!

Damn this bliss, it's 7.30pm and we are somewhere in Welford, moored up where the trees have formed a canopy above our boat. 4 other boats are far enough away not to be annoying and I'm sat here with wine, writing this diary waiting for dinner to cook, chicken and roasted veg if you care. There are only 2 downsides, 1 Roly lit joss sticks when I wasn't looking, I bloody hate those things, all clogging up your nostrils and boat with the scent of 'fake hippy seeks enlightenment'. The 2nd, we obviously have no internet or phone signal. Now why is it without a mobile I think something bad has happened to my loved ones, suddenly the director of bad shit calls up his or her team and says Jayne can't contact her family, quick send a massive drama to her home town. In my mind, I am out of range so daughter of 18 has fallen down a well accidentally taking 17yr stepson with her. Sister has taken children into a chasm of doom by mistake thinking it was an Asda. Brother has taken rest of the family including favorite Aunty into quick sand for a picnic. Friends have all ingested bleach having mistaken it for gin. How did we cope before everyone was contactable at every hour?! I want to stay here another day, not because I want to put any more people in mortal danger but because it's quiet and beautiful. Roly, who at present is also suffering the same 'outofrange-familydangerphobia' (possibly could have made that up) feels we should move on, let's see who wins. . . .

Travelling - Welford - to - Nowhere
Date - 27/07/14

We did stay of course and what a lovely place. I finally had a good night's sleep. We stopped the engine at 4pm yesterday, by the time we went to bed everything was cooler. Tonight will be the same, we've not moved the boat so no engine heat. We are also under a canopy of trees that has kept us nicely shaded.

We are going to have a BBQ here tonight and a pit fire, no idea why we need both but man and fire - he will be in his element, will probably dance round it. He is currently doing stuff with wood, lord knows what but he is happy.

Just saw an odd sight. A lady steering her narrow boat with her butt? Seriously she had the tiller wedged between the two ample cheeks, arms folded staring into the distance as she slowly motored along. She just shifted her hips when she wanted her arse to go left or right. Had she not considered what that sight looked like from behind?! "Roly, Roly" I hissed "look, look that woman has a stick up her arse".

Travelling - Welford - to - Maybe somewhere later
Date - 28/07/14

We are still under my canopy, I say mine because I've claimed it, may even paint double yellows here. Sadly, we may move on later though.

Last night at our lovely BBQ and much needed fire(?) I got two bites, now I will never win the window fight.

This morning I have been very busy reading then jigsaw, jigsaw then reading, then reading with the occasional passing of tools and holding of wires as he is busy fitting a solar panel. I better buy him a pub lunch when he's done.

When we were packing up to move onto Billow and subsequently unpacking, his mantra was 'keep it light, we have limited space'. Even with those words on a constant loop in my head I still managed to overdo it with clothes and had to send two small cases back. So how come he has what, by first count appears to be 27 tool boxes hidden in every nook and cranny. He likes fixing, tinkering and general pottering around with his tool in hand, pun intended, but pack light was the theme. I could have put books in those cranny's. Who needs 100 different screwdrivers anyway.

Two pigeons have been crashing about in my canopy, it's been going on so long I feel she should make her mind up. Either put out love before he runs out of energy or tell him he doesn't stand a chance and by flapping about in the trees after her, he is just coming across as desperate.

Travelling - Foxton Locks - to - Onwards
Date - 29/07/14

Finally saw my first live land creature last night, granted it was a rat but it made a nice change seeing it run into a bush rather than floating belly up surrounded by partying flies in the water.

We have 10 locks to do today as we make our way down Foxton. In true British style we are to queue, two up then we are sixth down. I didn't realise it got that busy, bet on the way back in winter it is deserted, for those I'll do the driving and he can do the locks. Brrrr.

Travelling - Foxton - to - The Ghetto
Date - 30/07/14

Today we are heading towards Leicester. Now four out of four people, when told we where we were heading went 'ohh either moor up on the central pontoon or drive straight through'. That's 100% of people if your maths is a bit rusty. This wasn't a Family Fortunes style survey, just canal folk exchanging travel plans. So I have to wonder, what did Leicester do to piss off the world of canal people. I've been to Leicester a few times, not my favorite place (sorry Leicester) but can't say I've noticed anything particularly terrifying there but perhaps the water is different. Roly has already hidden the precious gems and pots of gold in case some hooded youths attempt to board our vessel.

On our approach I have noticed more graffiti, or perhaps I'm looking for it. If we survive I shall write more later.

Mmmm, he & I may have words today, I was promised a more gentle day today. After this office girl, well I suppose at nearly 40 the term should be office woman but that just sounds old. Anyway I digress, this office girl had a lot of manual labour yesterday going down Foxton Locks, all whilst being gawped at by the hordes of picnickers and quizzed by an army of children covered in ice-cream and suntan lotion. Today since we set off, I've done nothing but locks and again, because we found someone to share with I'm not brave enough to drive with a captive audience so am opening & closing the damn locks, where is the pub I was promised!

We have just acquired some sweetcorn, not small enough to be baby corn and nowhere near big enough to be grown up corn, perhaps best described as toddler corn. A farmers field next to the lock was growing some, so we helped ourselves.

More scrumping than actual theft but if your reading this farmer, thank you for the ears and sorry you're missing a few.

Travelling - Kilby - to - The Ghetto
Date - 31/07/14

We never made it to Leicester, not because we were gunned down on approach but because the map readers sense of distance needs a little work. To be fair to him the locks do take hours out of your day.

As we are not sharing with anyone I'm driving and he is doing the locks. This is certainly the easy job! Holding her steady whilst he prepares the lock for me to drive into is the most difficult bit, I'll blame the wind as I'm all over the place. It's a miracle I've not ended up sideways. A few choice words have been exchanged and clearly he is an arsehole, of course it is not me being over sensitive to his Sargent Major style of barking instructions, it's just his general arseholeness. Hope his back aches tomorrow!

We are certainly getting closer to Leicester although, I have seen some stunning canalside gardens and some lovely new canal lilies, not the usual yellow but white and pink. I have also seen graffiti on and under every bridge. They have been tagged to within an inch of their life and I suspect that when we get closer to the centre the ducks that weren't mean enough to scare away the 'artists' will be tagged too.

Not been boat jacked yet but Leicester canal has, in addition to graffiti on every available surface, more water birds than I have ever seen. We had to negotiate round hordes of ducks and swans, they certainly seem to like it here. The locks have locks too, as in the working parts are only accessible with our trusty British Waterways key; we have to unlock the paddles that

9

control the water levels. Things must be bad if the Canal Trust think these hoodlums will steal the actual locks . . . Yes I know it's to prevent the little shits from flooding the canal, I just find the image of hooded youths carting away the entire lock, making a hasty get away on the BMW's amusing.

Another plentiful commodity floating in the Leicester canal, when we start to run short, is glass and aluminum. Mind you, you would have to separate the used nappies, plastic bags and other general waste to get to the cans and bottles.

Travelling - Leicester - to - River Soar
Date - 01/08/14

Nothing sinister happened in Leicester, the canal was just wasteland that's all. The people of Leicester are not to be feared so that's alright then. I will miss all that graffiti, didn't understand most of it granted, but two caught my eye. One was over a water overflow tunnel, some creative sole had drawn sharp teeth around the entrance with a set of eyes above. This person with too much time on their hands had created a rather impressive monster face, I liked it! The second was a sum, why would anyone graffiti maths on a lock? It is still puzzling me, what did this person gain from putting paint to steel to show the world (well at least other hoodlums and canal users) the sum $22 \div 7$? They hadn't even bothered to put the answer so I had to work it out for myself, 3.14 if you're interested. The answer is not quite Pi but according to Google, Pi and 22/7 feature together a lot, I won't bore you with the details, mainly because I can't be arsed to read it myself. So, is that the tag of Piscine Patel? Don't recall his adventures with Richard Parker covering Leicester and I have read that book a good few times, or is the mark a clue to something, like a secret rave?

At some point we were on the River Soar, no idea when it happened, as unhelpfully there are no motorway style signs saying you are leaving the Grand Union Canal. It was sort of just there, I thought wow this is a wide canal, turns out it was the river. Perhaps it's best I'm not captain!

Travelling - River Soar - to - Loughborough
Date - 02/08/14

Thought we would spend a few days in Barrow but for some reason Loughborough is calling to him, so at 4pm we set off on a two hour journey, you know what that means - the bedroom will be boiling. May have to bagsie the sofa if the engine doesn't cool down quick enough. What little we saw of Barrow was nice. It does seem though that quite a lot of the residents still believe in the dog poo fairy. I assume these are residents with dogs, if you don't have a dog the fairy is sort of irrelevant. Not since the '80's have I seen so much canine crap, all varying in size, shade and structure. So kind to leave that for us all to enjoy.

Oh the shame, silly Jayne I am beyond bloody embarrassed, Roly now has weeks if not months of ammunition. We moored up in Loughborough and walked to Tesco, finding the supermarket entrance via the carpark. After doing our shop, which should have just been milk but ended costing £45, we were drawn towards a nice looking Australian restaurant. On heading that way out of the car park a sign reminded me we only have 2 hours free parking. That is when I provided him with a year's worth of entertainment at my expense. I said 'Roly we need to get a ticket for the car'. The little bastard has not stopped laughing, he was actually bent over double with two bags shopping, (milk, plus extra's) laughing so hard tears flowed.

Travelling - Loughborough- to - Forwards
Date - 03/08/14

Today I've woken up with my first boat hangover, thank the lord for animated films and fizzy drinks. I blame the cheap red wine, it definitely had nothing to do with quantity, just quality. We moored up right outside a pub. It was a house that had been turned into a pub, from the outside it looked just like a regular home but with a pub sign hanging over the door. I'm not averse to a bit of quirky so thought we should give it a try. Roly however, thought it was too weird for him. Wasn't hard to persuade as he's not one to turn down a pint so I got him through the door.

He was right, it was weird, all downstairs house shaped, with a the bar in a living room sort of room. I'm not making any sense, just imagine your grans house with a bar stuck in the middle of it. Roly could have won an award for the speed at which he finished his drink. The place was all wood and brass and the wine was served in individual bottles. There were, when we arrived just a couple and the barman, that's it. They had a book swap shelf so I stayed for a 'few' whilst Roly scarpered back to the boat to tinker. I book swapped and read in peace, Roly tinkered in peace.

Travelling - Zouch - to - Kegworth
Date - 04/08/14

The good news is I am over my hangover, the bad news is I seem to have lost the ability to moor up well. Why has parking this thing suddenly escaped me? I was almost sideways this morning waiting for Roly to close the lock and climb back aboard. More practice is needed. Mind you, some people think I'm an expert. We lock shared earlier with some day trippers who had never done a lock before. They looked at me with big expectant owl eyes, well with over two weeks experience under my belt I straightened my headscarf, grabbed our good windlass and confidently lead the troops through two locks. Little did they know mostly I wing it and I still can't park.

Well I never, I have just seen and worked my first electric lock. I didn't know they existed. Manual labour was reduced to nil but the mental exercise involved had me stumped for a bit! 16 little buttons, 1 key and 1 big red button, it took a while to get my head round, initially I thought it was a Krypton Factor challenge. Actually once I'd sussed it out it was easy. Now I want them all to be like that.

Travelling - Sawley - to - Nowhere
Date - 05/08/14

Nothing to report today, we stayed at Sawley Marina as he wanted, no sorry, needed to go to the chandlery (a sort of nautical hardware shop) and they are closed Tuesdays. He is also waiting for a friend from Leicester to visit. The friend is bringing essentials. . . glue, lacquer, sealer, not a clue what he wants with all that but it keeps him busy and quiet!

Just watched the first two episodes of Breaking Bad, love it already. Know what I'll be doing next time there's a wet spell, thank goodness for box sets.

Travelling - Sawley - to - Somewhere else
Date - 06/08/14

Glad to be on the move again and I am pleased to report I had not lost the ability to moor up as previously thought, turns out steering a 57-foot canal boat in a cross wind is like eating rice with chopsticks, obviously not impossible but if you haven't had enough practice you are going to look like a fool. Now that I know that, I realise I'm an idiot for not noticing it before. Of course the wind plays a part, how could it not, we may weigh about a million tons but we are still floating.

I just saw, and I swear on the life of a large glass of Rioja this to be true, I just saw a terrapin sitting on a tree stump. Roly thinks I'm hallucinating or at the very least mistaking a rock for a terrapin. As he was in the kitchen making tea, his opinion doesn't count. I definitely saw a terrapin nonchalantly soaking up the sun on a stump, not a care in the world. Actually he or she may have been over thinking a huge problem, a regular reptile crisis, but if they were it was well hidden behind their carefree expression.

So, turns out the canal has a sense of humour, we have just dealt with a lock that is probably still snickering now. Roly drove Billow in and I got on with operating the lock. Every time I closed the gate and walked to the other end to open the paddles, the gate I just closed swung open, all the way open. It was like some slapstick comedy with me running backwards and forwards closing the gate & it slowly opening whilst I ran to get the opposite paddles open so it would stay closed, waving my windlass (big lock key thingy for opening paddles & letting water in/out) and swearing a lot. As the swearing didn't work we had to tie up Billow and both do it. Him holding the rebellious gate closed whilst I started emptying the water.

Travelling - Branston - to - Staying put
Date - 09/08/14

I mustn't laugh, I will bite the inside of my cheek to refrain from accidentally letting out a snicker or even a guffaw. The sight of Roly on his hands and knees, brandishing the bleach spray wearing disposal gloves and spitting out expletives like a true sailor. The reason for his small melt down is dog poo. One ignorant fairy believer left a lovely little bundle for Roly to step in, then walk through the boat. Of course I'm glad it wasn't me, wouldn't have been half as funny then! Spray bleach, swear and scrub, then to mix it up swear, bleach, swear and scrub. I've not seen the floor look so clean. He paused from scrubbing and swearing to glare at a passing dog. Couldn't hold that laugh in, he is on his hands and knees still, giving a golden retriever a dirty look through the porthole, this poor canine wanders passed with a soppy happy grin on it's face oblivious to the hatred being aimed at him.

We just nipped to Barton Marina, I say nipped but actually, on a boat you don't nip anywhere. It will take several hours there & unsurprisingly several hours back including a stop to empty the loo. We have guests coming and one doesn't want a full loo with visitors! We get to Barton Marina, eventually and what a lovely marina it is too. A nice pub, some shops and even a cinema. Obviously we (I) had to have a nose in all the shops, it was almost a little designer label village, Joules, Radley etc and my new favorite thing since being on the boat, a farm shop. I am a sucker for a farm shop. Love all the unusual stuff, overpriced pretty pasta, local meats and cheeses. I even go mad for the vegetables, is there such a thing as high end groceries? A posher carrot, a classier potato.

When we finished shopping we headed off to the sanitary area (still not my job). £1.50 was required to use the facilities we were duly informed. So far we haven't had to pay anything to empty the cassette so at first I thought it was an attempt at humour. Nope, turns out this guy really wanted £1.50. If you are going to charge, do actually charge. What is the point of £1.50, it won't even get you a coffee, or some fancy pasta! Charge a real amount and do more than just unlock the door.

Travelling - Branston - to - Barton
Date - 11/08/14

Had egg and soldiers for breakfast, soldiers with duck eggs purchased at the farms shops I can never resist. As I've spent the last three weeks feeding every duck within bread chucking distance, guilt joined me for breakfast. It didn't even cross my mind as I added the eggs to my basket, but now, lobbing the top off so my soldier could gain access I am feeling less than good about myself. I had to keep my eyes downcast whilst eating furtively, so as not to spot any possible relatives hoping for snacks at our boat. I think I'll bypass the duck eggs next time, not so many chickens on the canal and no one needs guilt spoiling their breakfast.

Had the family over today, it was lovely see them. Roly made us go in the 'Mug Tug', a boat that does children's pottery painting. .You know the sort, you pick a piece, mug, trinket holder, money box etc then kids throw as much paint at it as possible before presenting it to Nonna for her birthday as a one off masterpiece. As it is the school holidays this narrow boat was stuffed full of children eagerly decorating ornaments to rival Wedgewood and slap bang in the middle of this rainbow chaos is a table with us four. . . now the problem with that is, yes we may have taken our children for a fun activity whist they visited mum and dad, but our kids are 17 and 18 so technically there were four adults squashed onto child sized table and chairs. I tried to excuse myself for two reasons, the first being I paint like a Dulux tin has sneezed and second I would much rather have been shopping than pretending I was five. However, Chloe, my 18yr quite rightly pointed out if she had to do it, so did I. I picked the tiniest, simplest thing I could find, a flower fridge magnet. 1 centre, 6 petals, in and out as quickly as possible. Even with that most modest thing the owner came over and pointed out I'd missed a bit, yes thanks for that. A little boy restrained in a high chair on the table next to us kept shouting 'out out', me too my friend, me too.

Travelling - Barton Marina - to - West
Date - 12/08/14

Ran the tap to wash up this morning and the water was a lovely coral pink, a little worrying. We don't drink the water, the boat has a 200 gallon tank and I don't like the idea of 200 gallons just sitting there going stale, I may as well stick a straw in my pond at home and have a slurp. Now I'm not convinced I want to wash up with it and definitely do not want to brush my teeth with it dispute its attractive hue. Roly thinks it's rust and he is wearing a concerned expression, I shall look into local hotels as I may have to make a quick getaway if he starts pulling the boat apart to get to the tank!

Saw some interesting wildlife today, a yellow and black caterpillar followed by a hedgehog. Well, the caterpillar I nearly drowned and the hedgehog couldn't have been anymore dead. We were mooring up to go to the pub, quite standard for us. Crawling along a bramble overhanging the canal was a caterpillar disguised as a bee, perhaps he had been to a fancy dress party. Turns out it was the caterpillar of the cinnabar moth, who is indeed yellow and black. As the daft creature was heading for a swim he probably wasn't expecting, I thought I'd do my conservation duty and, with no thought to my own safety (he could have been vicious, a larva serial killer or something) I lent down and grabbed a leaf to pull the rogue vine in. It seems the leaf I grabbed had no desire to stay attached to its host and it came away in my hand. Sadly, this launched the unsuspecting creature head first into the canal. Before shock set in, I quickly scooped him out the water and

17

shoved him into some undergrowth, praying he hadn't had time to notice it was me that had ruined his day.

The hedgehog, I think is worth a mention because in all of the roadkill I have seen, I have never ever seen one as flat as this. It was paper thin! I can only assume this road we were walking alongside, whilst heading for the pub previously mentioned in the nice village of Handsacre, either regularly had tanks drive through or the locals deliberately aimed for this hedgehog every time they used this road. I believe you could have inserted him into your inkjet and printed your C.V on him, obviously you would need to use a different coloured ink, black wouldn't show up well.

Travelling - Handsacre - to - Not far
Date - 13/08/14

We have just been over our first aqueduct, the concept of a canal crossing over something, in this case a river had me quite excited, sad as I am. In reality I found it rather disappointing, not sure what I was expecting to happen but nothing exciting did happen, unsurprisingly it felt exactly the same as not being on an aqueduct. Hope the huge one in wales proves more fulfilling.

Obviously on our journey we have seen an array of waterfowl, mallards, swans, coots, Canadian geese, moorhens etc plus all their associated offspring, the only one I know the name of is cygnet so I'll call the rest baby ducks. I have also seen some white ones and some black ones with white bits; no idea what they are but Google informs me they are the domestic duck and the American black, but of course the internet could be lying. I have also seen, what I have decided, no doubt in my ignorance are mixed race ducks. A beautiful mixture of all sorts.

Most of the ducks seem to share parenting Swans, I know mate for life, the others seem to have 2 adults per collection of young, but not the mallards, why are they different? For every 50 or so females, hen ducks I see only 1 drake. There are certainly mallard ducklings, so either the drake has a huge harem of concubines or once the spring deed is done, masses of soon to be fathers migrate to a mallard gentlemen's club until the ducklings are no longer at that annoying baby stage.

Travelling - Wildwood - to - A bit further
Date - 14/08/14

Our water last night turned a bright orange colour, after checking we hadn't accidently filled up with Irn Bru instead of water, we started to look up the services of a boat fixey person within the vicinity sadly no one was available till morning. Then the taps started spluttering and spitting, so Roly made a dipstick and wrapped some kitchen towel round the end to see if the water tank had anything to offer by way of explanation, turns out we had run the tank dry, oop's. Seeing the bright colours cascading out of the tap as the water came forth from the bowels of a 200 gallon stagnant tank, just reassured me I was right not to drink the tap water. We are off to find a water point, maybe that will fix the problem?!

Since we started our journey I have been keeping old food, not for any keepsake purposes or a weird hording habit but to dispose of by feeding the animals. Stale bread and left over gingerbread men (don't tell my nephew, he saved that especially for me) for the ducks and swans, the rest to throw into the hedgerows and undergrowth for hedgehogs, birds and squirrels etc. Roly hugely disapproves of this act as he thinks I'm littering and also encouraging rats onto the boat. My argument is that an overripe banana or some left over beans does not constitute litter. Either a very lucky animal will find his dinner has been delivered to him or it will decompose thus fertilising the soil. As I never leave a forwarding address or the name of our boat on the food scraps, I am pretty confident the rats are not about to come knocking, begging bowl out asking 'please sir, can I have some more'. I hope I am doing no harm by disposing of food this way but in case, here is my apology to all the flora or fauna that ever had an apple core land on them.

Oh dear, water tank problem worsening. We came to a boat yard before a water point so Roly thought we should stop and ask. Unfortunately, the guys face did that thing usually reserved for mechanics, he pursed his lips and on just one side of his face he looked like he had sucked a lemon then he uttered the dreaded words 'don't look good mate'. He followed that up with 'I'm off to lunch if you take off the water tank top hatch we'll look when I'm back'. One hour, several screwdrivers, one hammer, one mallet, two chisels, an outstanding collection of swear words and one blow torch later and not one single screw had budged. I think, after being comfortably snuggled down for the last twelve years since Billow was built, those eight screws have no intention of yielding to some crazy faced fool swearing at them whilst brandishing big scary tools.

Travelling - Penkridge - to - Nowhere fast
Date - 15/08/14

Thought we should stay in Penkridge for a bit so Roly can continue attacking the lid to the water tank. He is going to drill out the screw heads apparently.

On our return from a visit to the village shops today we heard a loud bellowing from a man moored up behind us.

Turns out some selfish sod has left dog mess just where he has moored. Now Roly handles this by giving passing canines dirty looks, but this guy, no. This guy shouts at the top of his lungs he would like to stick a knife in them, not sure if he means the dog or the owner but either is worrying! As he looks like he may be staying I think I shall set up a trip wire around Billow before I go to bed tonight, just in case he is unable to locate the villains that caused his wrath.

Still talking about toilet business (that seems to feature a lot in this diary), most of us are aware the dog poo fairy doesn't exist, but I'm starting to think the canal side toilet fairy may actually be true. All along the canal routes are toilet emptying facilities, rubbish bins and toilet blocks. The magical British Water Ways key open up these toilets. Granted the less than savoury public can't gain access and write on the walls or steal the loo roll, but every one of these I've used have been lovely, if you can actually call a WC lovely. Far exceeding a lot of pub and club toilets I've visited. They are always fully stocked and weirdly all have smelt nice, does a fairy squirt a bit of febreeze just before I enter I wonder? The only downside to these places that I have found so far is the books left for book swap. It is all Mills & Boon everywhere, perhaps I should try the men's.

Travelling - Still in Penkridge
Date - 16/08/14

Roly finally broke into the water tank, he had to drill out all eight screws, they fought well, but he finally beat them. Peering down into our tank was an interesting sight, like some weird ginger secret cave. Thankfully there were no mutated multi eyed life forms squelching around in there, just some elaborate stalagmites. So very glad I never drank from that. We spent a wonderful afternoon bucket emptying the thing, watching the water get darker and get darker. Such lovely shades of orange reminiscent of a romantic sunset, oddly neither of us were moved by that; the dirt, grim, sweat and lower back ache saw to that. With no water and skin the colour of an umpa lumpa we decided to treat ourselves to a night in a hotel. After checking availability and that the hotel actually had a bath, we parted with £130 for the privilege. At that price I had high hopes and dashed about the boat packing the essentials Radox, wine and a scented tealight. I didn't opt for a 'real' candle in case I set off the smoke detectors and got kicked out mid soak. To say I was looking forward to this would have been a massive understatement. As much as I am enjoying this adventure, I massively miss my bath. Also our bed on board was built for space efficiency rather than comfort. Thankfully at 5'1 and 5'5 we were built for the bed, but a night in a double bed was not to be sniffed at.

Two short, slightly less orange (got to love a wet wipe) umpa lumpas rocked up to our overnight accommodation. We got overexcited about the size of the bed, it was only two singles shoved together but as we have been sleeping in a space just over 6' x 4' this bed seemed immense, Roly went so far as to wonder if each side had its own postcode and did snow angels on the duvet. The standards of the hotel did not live up to its price tag, I have no objection to paying the right price for the right place as a night away could be an indulgence but £130 should not include peeling wallpaper, chipped paint, a bit of an unidentified pong and no free biscuits! Bath and bed were included in the price and that's what I needed most.

Trying not to be a negative nelly but when I asked if the room had a bath, I wasn't asking on behalf of Flat Stanley, I was asking for me - a normal sized short person. That was not a bath, that was an oversized shower tray. It would have been suitable for a hobbit, if they had smaller feet. It was shallow, narrow and short and that's coming from me! I am one determined woman, so in went the water, hot enough to scald not worth having a bath unless it's hot enough to boil eggs, the Radox to create a mountain of bubbles and a teeny tiny tealight, not in the water obviously, stationed bath side next to my wine and book. I wish I could say I slid into my bubblious heaven, but in reality I just sort of contorted into it. With regular turning, like that of a grilling sausage, I managed to stay in for an hour.

Travelling - Penkridge still
Date - 17/08/14

Roly has spent most of today folded up inside the water tank, that wasn't some bizarre punishment for snoring last night in our grown up bed, he is inside to scrape the rust off the floor and walls before it can be treated. I'm pretty sure it isn't the nicest thing he has done since we set sail.

My role is to pass him equipment and drinks and to treat the underside of the lid. Now, when I paint I tend to wear a lot of it, I'm like some sort of wet paint magnet and bitumen apparently is nasty sticky stuff. So after I had scrapped and wire brushed the lid, I donned rubber gloves and overalls, seriously for a square of metal 18 x 180 I looked like I was ready for chemical warfare. After I finished the first coat I wrapped my baby roller and tray in plastic like a good girl and because my gloved fingers were sticky I left the lid and tin alone in anticipation of coat two.

A little while later Roly emerged from his hole to have a beer and stretch out, I don't know if being bent over double for so long effected how his legs worked or if he just suddenly forgot how to move but in classic slow motion comedy effect, he stumbled getting out of the cratch (that really is the name for the front covered bit of a boat)! In falling he spilt beer on my newly painted lid, himself and into the open tin of bitumen then to finish his 'baby gazelle taking first steps' move, he kicked over the bitumen beer coating the unsuspecting grass and his boots. Thankfully I was too shocked to laugh immediately because before he had even recovered from his acrobatic display, steam was already coming out of his ears. Solemnly, whilst really biting the inside of my lip hard I asked if he was ok, he confirmed that yes, he was, then proceeded to berate himself on such a foolish act. What he really wanted to say was 'stupid woman, why did you not put the lid on properly and why did your stupid arse leave the tin there anyway' insert any random swear words. We now have no bitumen and the chandlers isn't open Sunday, separate hotels perhaps tonight?!

Travelling - Still Penkridge
Date - 18/08/14

We chose a different hotel for last night, half the price. Wow what a difference, for our £65 we got lovely decor with no peeling or chipping in sight. Absolutely no bad odor and of course, a little packet of free biscuits. More importantly the bath lived up to its name and my whole body could bathe in it. I am bitter enough about the contrasting experiences to name and shame. Now, if you ever find yourself in Penkridge do stay in The Littleton Arms, for the price you will have a lovely night away. Oddly the morning fry up didn't come with beans, but I for one can live with that. If on the other hand you have money to burn, zero standards and can't live without beans on your brekkie then I suggest throwing your cash at The Mercure Hatherton House Hotel, obviously don't bother packing your Radox, unless you are an actual pixie.

Travelling - Penkridge - to - Onwards
Date - 19/08/14

Today is a good day and a bad day. We are finally leaving Penkridge, a lovely village but we were champing at the bit to get going however, it is chucking it down and we have a lot of locks to do. This is our first rainy day on the move, not the nicest but as it isn't freezing yet I'll save my moaning for winter! To be fair, I am only going above deck when it's lock time, so Roly has it tougher. I'll keep him going with a constant supply of tea.

The good/bad aspect isn't the weather, or us on the move. It is because today is my little girl's birthday, I say little, she is taller than me and has turned 18 today. I wish I was home to watch her open her presents however, seeing as she is away with her friend, being at home would be just as useful as being on our boat! We had a birthday picnic when she visited with the family last week. Cake, candles and prosecco. She couldn't be persuaded or bribed into opening any of her presents as she wanted to wait until her actual birthday, she even took the Bollinger unopened, gutted! I shall just have to bombard her with phone calls all day until she tells me to go away!

We performed our first recovery mission, sadly nothing as exciting as saving lives or rescuing puppies. A moored up boat we passed must have gotten bored with its existing scenery and decided to head off on its own seeking adventure and perhaps companionship. Far be it from me to appoint us fun police but seeing as only the front rope had snapped and the craft was only going to end up sideways we decided we should intervene. On re-tying the front rope we discovered that it wasn't the first time this boat had tried to escape, it had more knots in it than long hair caught in a gale. So apologies for crushing your dream Aragon (for that was the name of the boat) and I hope your owners invest in some new rope.

We had dinner in a nice pub, a Vintage Inn chain. I only worked that out after musing over why their menu offered vintage pies and vintage hunters chicken. I saw no need for the pies to declare themselves vintage, the fillings sounded modern and the pastry appeared fresh. Turns out they weren't being pretentious, they were just branding their pies. Roly's starter was pâté and as usual the bread to pâté ratio was imbalanced, we had the audacity to ask for more, so they charged us one whole pound for it. Who charges for a bit more bread with your starter? When we had finished giggling over the ludicrousness of no free bread an older couple took the table behind Roly. My oh my, I have never seen eyebrows like it, they were fascinating. He had eyebrows that, if it wasn't for the resemblance to steel wool and them not being eyelashes could have modelled mascara for a living. Those luscious grey appendages grew up out and round, in my day to try and achieve anything resembling those great fluttery things on my eyelashes I had to use eyelash curlers and a buildup of mascara thick enough to be called rope. Nowadays the kids seem to use superglue and peacock feathers. How his companion and for convenience I shall call her his wife had not noticed, surely if she got within 5 foot of him those things would get all tangled up in her hair and clothes? If he was reluctant to do a bit of self grooming, she could have gone at those eyebrows with a pair of garden shears whilst he was sleeping and he wouldn't have noticed. If Roly gets one stray nose or eyebrow hair, I'm at him like a monkey grooming her mate. He hates it but if I let that one annoying hair slide, next thing you know I'll be discussing the price of extra starter bread with a human wire brush and the young couple behind us would be wondering how I failed to notice all the overgrown hedgerow protruding from my husband's face!

Travelling - Coven - to - Closer to Wales
Date - 20/08/14

I didn't know there was a place called Coven until we pitched up at it. I just want to add the word 'witches' to it, I suppose they must get that a lot. Thankfully I am not a graffiti artist/vandal, nor did I actually see the 'Welcome to Coven' sign.

Whilst I sat in the sun (of course it stopped raining when we finished the locks) doing a jigsaw Roly went off foraging for wood, he is obsessed with the stuff. He is collecting it for winter, quite right, but also because 'I might make something out of that'. If I don't keep an eye on him he would fill this boat with things that might come in handy and wood, lots and lots of wood.

We have seen two kingfishers today, well we think they were kingfishers as they are so fast it could just be blue dots dancing before our eyes! I can't even think about getting the camera out before they are gone, a flash of blue just darts into the trees. Slow down, let me get a look at you. Perfect timing really, I was starting to get a bit bored of ducks, no offence Donald. Mind you, at least you get a good look at ducks, they are not shy in showing off for bread. Even the herons give us a regal stare as we pass by but no, not the kingfisher he is not interested at all.

Bloody hell Wolverhampton must be the area for kingfishers, we have just seen our third one today. This one got close enough to let us see his striking blue and orange but not so close as to photograph him. He just kept flying two or three trees ahead of us. We could just make him out on the branch but if we had have clicked the shutter it would have been one of those pictures that when showing your friends you point going 'there is a kingfisher, can you see that speck of blue' and they can't even bring themselves to at least pretend to see it.

For some reason I thought kingfishers were bigger, they are actually quite small.

Travelling - Canalside somewhere
Date - 21/08/14

And so it begins, my hoarder husband has started to sneak wood onto the roof. I told him at the beginning I didn't want to live on a boat with crap littering the top, I've seen loads and I think they spoil a boat. Tyres, branches, spare fenders, empty plant pots, brushes, bicycles and even half a loo, I could go on and on! It ruins my romantic image of boating, so if it doesn't fit in the cratch (that's the front conservatory bit if you like, not a euphemism) we aren't keeping it! God I'm harsh but if left to his own devices our boat would end up like Steptoe & Son's yard, this is a man who kept a spare kettle and a spare DVD player. . . just in case.

We've moored up somewhere on the Shropshire canal, maybe 8 or 10 miles from Market Drayton. It was getting quite nippy in the wind and rain, yes I know it is only August. Plus, with the foragers collection of wood building up he is bursting to start a fire for the first time in our log burner. The squirrel log burner he keeps telling me excitedly, apparently a good one, no, no idea either. So we have an evening in front of the fire, curled up watching a DVD, a practice run for winter.

I've spotted a poster that is advertising a canal boat market on for the next few days. I AM THERE, shopping, on boats, it would be rude not too! Expect to come home laden with local chutneys, honey and a bohemian outfit.

Travelling - Market Drayton -to - Nowhere
Date - 22/08/14

Up early to 'dash' to the floating market, if you can call walking pace dashing. Five locks close together, so I drove and Roly did the gates. Three of the five were standard 'I can do these confidently now' locks but two came down to exit at great gushing outlets of water. Right outside the gate, on leaving was a strong sideways current. Oh here we go! The first one of the awkward two I negotiated, I wouldn't go so far as to say confidently, more like on nervous tiptoe with many a high pitched ohh and argh and possibly with one eye closed, but that method seemed to work and Billow actually stayed straight. The second one didn't go quite so well. I blame the fact I had to pick Roly up from the towpath this time. So I exit the lock, negotiate the front end past the torrent. Forgetting I needed to counteract the great side swipe to the rear of the boat I started to steer into the bank to pick up the labourer, the gushing water started shoving the rear in the opposite direction, fast! I won't bore you with the details, not because I'm embarrassed of course. Suffice to say I ended up sideways, forgetting which was my right and left, hopping up and down shouting at Roly to Help Help. I possibly may have cried a little bit too.

We did get to Market Drayton for the market, no thanks to my sideways driving, but it wasn't worth stopping. Approximately six boats had their wares out. Of the six, two were tea & bacon butty boats and one sold fenders and buttons (the rope bits that hang down the sides and sit on the front and rear of the boat - to protect it from idiot sideways drivers bashing it into things). That leaves three, no flies on me. There was a boat selling wood sculptures, with the artist sat canalside polishing a piece, I knew she was the artist, not because of the wood carving in her hand but because of her attire. Only an artist could confidently sit in a deckchair wearing pink and white fluffy slippers, tie-dye 'festival' trousers (a bit MC Hammer, you know the one's), a crochet cardy and then the pièce de résistance - a black bowler hat. Now, dressed like that one would expect a bohemian attitude to her pricing, but £750 for a 10" tall bit of polished wood, seriously! I had to check for a decimal point. Roly's wood obsession may come in handy if we run out of cash, whip off the bark, sand and varnish it, then whack it on a plinth and sell it for just 10% of what she was charging. I appreciate I sound very cocksure for someone without an ounce of artistic flair, but the man I married has oodles so I will be arrogant on his behalf.

Travelling - Market Drayton -to - Still here
Date - 23/08/14

The gods of ornithology have delivered me a change to the mallard today, had to google them but today I fed mandarin. Both male and female, nice colours, weird eyes. Is that what we eat at when putting away crispy shredded duck? There was also a solitary muscovy duck, this poor creature looks like Frankenstein built a new breed from a goose, a blackbird and a turkey, no wonder he was on his own.

We decided to eat at a Chinese restaurant tonight, the food was very good, as were the two bottles of wine we managed to put away! During dinner we were busy guessing which year songs were released (he was winning 3, 2), when a group of six walked in and were seated at a table close. They were the poshest sounding people I have ever heard, well technically four of them had humongous plums in mouths, mummy daddy, army boy son and daughter. The other two I did not hear speak once. They could have been mute but as no sign language sprinkled the conversation I suspect they were just unable to get a word in. I so wish I had a dictaphone, their entire conversation was enthralling and comedy upper class, so entertaining I forgot about our competition and sat transfixed, discreetly of course. I waited for daddy, for that is what his grown up children called him to bellow 'what what' and 'tallyho' at any moment. I was hooked the moment I heard the son say the word tuck. For me, tuck only ever existed in Enid Blyton books or Roald Dahl's autobiography, but no it is amongst us. He said the words 'they loved it when he bought in Cadbury animal crackers for tuck'. I was so excited I nearly abandoned Roly to scooch over to join their table. No need I could hear perfectly well even if I had to keep shh'ing the hubby. I won't write their entire conversation because sadly I cannot remember it word for word, but what I made a note of, yes I really did take notes I shall tell you about. Interestingly the vicar and his son are coming for tea, again I didn't realise that existed outside of period dramas, anyway the vicar's son is only 16 so they were discussing whether or not to ask permission from the lads dad, the man of cloth, to give him a glass of champagne or whether to take the initiative and give him a glass anyway. They all seemed in favour of getting the kid plastered. Parents and offspring then had a debate about whether Japan or Vietnam did the best pancakes for duck, mummy had the last word on that one because the chef comes out and makes them fresh for you in Saigon, Vietnam wins. Finally, one last anecdote as this is my diary not theirs. They discussed the merits of ballet over opera, a quick conversation as they all unanimously concluded that opera was for people with superiority complexes, unless of course you are listening to opera at home, in which case that's ok. I really wish I had a large cage or tank on me at that time. I know kidnapping is wrong, but I really really wanted to take the four of them home with me as some sort of conversation pets and, maybe the other silent two could have had a fun evening listening to each other's voices for a change. Now I don't want you thinking that

Roly and I had stumbled across an exclusive award winning Chinese restaurant where you have to book six months in advance or know the chef by name to get in, no we had enjoyed fine food and two bottles of house red for less than £60 inc tip, bargain! And yes mummy had the house wine too.

Travelling - There and - to - Back again
Date - 24/08/14

My stepson Dylan is 17 today, miss him but he is at work so wouldn't be seeing him anyway. He had his presents and cake when they visited recently as well, that kept him happy.

I got a phone call at 2am this morning from my 18yr old daughter, only heard music, no actual speaking and when I tried to call her back, no answer. In my head I knew she was fine as we had exchanged texts just before I went to bed. She had a friend round and was telling me that she had been ID'd buying the 'Shardonnay', which, as she was now legal she was quite excited about, after berating her for the spelling, I mean her mother has drunk enough of it for her to have noticed the letter C, I fell asleep. So I knew she was okay really and that it was an accidental call, but even so, I lay awake whittling a little. So imagine my delight when she called back at 3.30am and proceeded to tell me all about her impromptu first night out into town, all whilst she was munching on pizza. That really was Chloe's first night out on the town, in the preceding couple of years, despite encouragement from me she had never tried to seek out fake ID and had no interest in 'town', I really was starting to get worried about her! So after hearing all about her night and checking Caitlin got home safe too, we ended the call. I then stayed wide awake till way past 4.30am, the joys of motherhood.

We had friends and their kids visit today, it was a lovely day. We took them up the canal and back again so their boys could have a go at locks and play at being captains. They were more impressed with Roly's flashing LED lights, yes they are as chavy as they sound. He fit a strip under the gunnel (it's a bit like a dado rail) in the living room and tried to sell it to me as 'mood lighting'. Because you can change the colours and set them to various flashing speeds the boys loved them and spent literally the whole day arguing over whose turn it was with the remote control. Incidentally, whenever you change the channel on the TV it alters the colour of the lighting, such fun! The boys did leave the lights alone long enough to enjoy other things too, the roof, binoculars and of course the locks had them captivated. The little girl, not so much. Milk, crying and sleeping seemed to be her thing, but I suppose that's babies for you. I had some lunch in, suitable for busy excited children, mini sausage rolls, cookies - highly nutritious stuff. As I was putting the pizzas in the pre-heated oven the eldest asked if he could do it, not being a person that usually puts small boys in danger I told him to ask his mum, thus washing my hands of any responsibility should he decide to throw himself into the oven. Mum said yes, so he delicately scooped up a little cheese and tomato pizza, carried it carefully to the furnace and yes, you guessed it, his fingers touched the hot shelf. Like a pro I lifted him up onto the draining board and ran his fingers under the tap, unaware that my fast ninja like reaction had knocked the pizza box onto the lit hob the kettle was boiling on, chaos reigned! After putting out the fire and depositing the now drenched child back on the floor we had lunch!

Travelling - Market Drayton - to - Audlem
Date - 25/08/14

We have another friend coming tomorrow, although when she called at 9am this morning after a night out in Ramsgate she was still hammered and contemplating just carrying on, so the chances of seeing her are slimmer than a cigarette paper.

Thought we would make the journey anyway as there were 15 locks to get through. Both of us have it down to a fine art, hopping on and off a moving Billow to swap chores on lock duty. It was raining but without the wind it was quite pleasant. We had great fun actually, even when I spectacularly slid on my arse. It was my turn to open/close the lock and, rather than cross over to the other side of the lock where the stairs were I thought I would be a smart arse and just sort of skid down the smooth concrete on the side of the canal I was already on, surfer style. Clever Jayne, really clever, unsurprisingly that didn't go to plan and I fell butt first onto the muddy slope & slid all the way down on my derrière, the seat of my jeans were oaked in thick mud by the time I came to a stop, Roly laughed so hard he nearly gave himself a hernia.

Travelling - Nantwich - to - The Llangollen canal
Date - 28/08/14

Our friend Jenny, hardcore as she is did arrive, so we drank far too much wine, played music on the stereo a little too loud and all ended up doing the ice bucket challenge, after sending Roly to the Co-op to buy bags of ice of course. Following that, yesterday was a hangover write off.

Today we made it to the Llangollen canal, a steep flight of four locks. There I saw a mole and a rat, I hadn't flipped into some wind in the willows parallel universe, these two, although clearly inseparable were very much dead. It was odd looking into the water at them, they were caught in the lock current, the rat was swirling round face down and the mole, oddly was dancing alongside his companion butt up. No idea why he was in the dive position, maybe he had died wearing an incredibly heavy hat.

We chose to moor up at bridge 3 on the promise of 'award winning' ice-cream, both our map book and posters promised good things. The bridge had a map and a vague reference to a ten to twenty minute walk, so off we trot. Three fields and five styles later, the realisation came that we had gone from a nice leisurely walk, to a trek with some orienteering thrown in for good measure, all for ice cream, usually I only do that for wine or cheese. I spotted something through the trees, was it an ice cream shop? No, I saw a tall structure and said to Roly, that looks like a Dalek. Sure enough, two minutes later onto the home straight and we saw what it was, a giant Dalek. Whilst pondering the reason someone would put a giant Doctor Who extraterrestrial in the middle of a field we stumbled upon our destination Snugburys ice cream place. Turns out the Dalek was put there by Snugburys. 35ft high straw and steel structure that moved its head and talked, well it just said exterminate, quite a limited vocabulary if you ask me. Incidentally the ice cream was worth the walk, my two scoop was turkish delight & ginger and honey. The place also had some goats and pigs, Snugburys noticeboard showed photographs of the previous giant straw sculptures built but more importantly that they had piglets for sale. Quite unfairly Roly point blank refused to let me buy on. Mean.

Travelling - Bridge 3 on the Llangollen canal - to - A bit further
Date - 29/08/14

We were planning to stay here for a few days, but at 5pm Roly decided he wanted to head to the next town and have a pint in a pub (as we are fully stocked with liquid of the dehydrating kind, I suspect the urgent need to move came from the discovery his tobacco supply was in danger of running out). As a previous smoker, although never nasty roll ups, I knew his worry . . . but as a reformed smoker, I preach and think he should quit, hence the ruse of a pint. By the time we got to the village shop it was, of course shut, but he had enough to get through the evening so we headed for the local for some food & a much needed drink, confident Roly could last the night. The evening accidentally went on until closing, I entirely blame the couple on the table next to us. When we initially arrived the place was heaving and the only table available was technically a table of four with a couple already sat on half of it. Their food had just arrived when we were seated, so in true British style we ignored each other. The lady was tiny, I mean not just bird like but hummingbird like and she had the biggest mountain of food I have ever seen. Two slices of black pudding the circumference of a pint glass and two giant pork chops, surrounded by an immense pile of veg and mash. Where was this minuscule woman going to put all that food, turns out after skimming just the top off her husband finished it. Polite conversation started after they heard us talking about Billow and our next destination. They have a boat too, so we exchanged boat into and canal routes. Half way through dinner a guy came round with quiz sheets, Roly and I declined still intent on going home after we had been fed and watered, but the couple next to us took one. After dinner the conversation and the wine flowed, so we stayed for another. Then the quiz started and we got stuck in 'helping' with their quiz, then the dingbats that followed and then play your cards right. We rolled out of the pub after closing waving goodbye to our new nameless friends.

Travelling - Wrenbury - to - Nowhere
Date - 30/08/14

Feeling a little worse for wear today, so we decided to stay. The weather looked good so later we could sit canalside, him painting, me reading.

When we are ready to go we have two lift bridges to do. One mechanical and one electronic, wonder how that will go?!

After a pub lunch (yes, we do seem to live in these places), we walked back to the boat to start our afternoon outdoor activities and it started to hammer it down, so I am inside writing, whilst Roly is watching Pineapple Express. I must stop though as I'm getting distracted laughing so much.

Travelling - Wrenbury - to - Onwards
Date - 31/08/14

I'm starting to think Roly has got cabin fever, as again, this morning, he was itching to go. May have to google symptoms when we have signal. He can't outrun it whatever it is, especially not at this speed.

Have done both lift bridges now. Sad as I am, I made us wait until all the other boats had gone through so that I could do them by myself. The first one was not very interesting, just a mechanical lift bridge for a foot path, it made a change from locks though. Lift bridge number two was much more exciting!

It was a road that needed lifting when boats passed. You turned your magical all opening Waterways keys in the operating box and the warning alarm sounded, like a police siren, signal warning lights also started flashing. Next you needed to close the road barrier, with its massive red Stop sign, because the alarm, red lights and soon to be missing road weren't enough to warn motorists. Once the warning barrier was in place you could either run or take a leisurely stroll back across to the function box and press the all important raise bridge button. Oh, the power I felt surging through my fingertips, raising a whole piece of road skywards, holding up traffic with my magnificence, controlling that little bit of Wrenbury on a Sunday morning. Okay the words power and magnificence may have been an exaggeration, bit I still enjoyed it.

We just sailed, motored, drove (no idea what the correct boating term is) past a massive fallen tree and Roly noticed someone had already started chainsawing off huge chunks of it, of course we had to reverse back so he could hop off and grab a bit, sadly it wasn't that simple. I took the middle rope, so he could go and find the perfect specimen, now when you put a boat into neutral it carries on a little way in the direction you were travelling, in this case backwards and you hang onto the middle rope to bring it to a stop, no brakes see. Unbeknown to me Roly, in his excitement had actually left Billow in reverse. He is oblivious, bent down engrossed in a pile of dead tree and I'm hanging onto this rope wondering why she won't stop. with a shout of 'help Roly I can't stop', he looks up and spots me stumbling around getting further and further away from him, I don't think we could have looked any more novice if we tried. Roly had to run Usain Bolt style to get to the back of the boat and climb aboard. After he has driven forwards again I made him check it was out of gear before he was allowed to go and drool over the tree carcass. The bit he rolled to the front of the boat, was of course the largest and no doubt he will have hurt his back trying to get it in, he has no idea what he is going to make with it yet, I do, a mess!

Travelling - Whitchurch - to - Somewhere else
Date - 01/09/14

Yet another pub lunch and I heard an interesting song whilst waiting for my tuna sandwich. A brother and sister were squabbling over whose turn it was to dangle off some piece of play equipment or other, when the male of the duo broke into sweet angelic song, the choir boy, unbroken voice kind and serenaded his sibling with 'ugly big fart wart, ugly big fat wart'. What a brilliant put down, where did he hear that or did he make it up? I wanted to ask him about it and congratulate him on his interesting imagination, perhaps he was a descendant of Roald Dahl. I thought better of it as one should never approach strange children at play, who knows what weirdos they may turn out to be and as a second thought it may have made his sister feel worse.

Travelling - Ellesmere - to - Up the canal a bit
Date - 02/09/14

We finally got to sample some damsons today, I'm loving this foraging lark. We had them for breakfast with a shop bought grapefruit so hardly living wild but still, eating free stuff is tastier than paying for it. I am also determined to get my sticky fingers on some grown up sweetcorn, around here it's not quite ripe yet so my criminal activity needs to wait.

Almost lost a flip flop earlier, I say almost, it did actually go in the canal but as it floated instead of sinking we managed to retrieve it. Roly of course, gave it the 'I told you so'. I've been wearing my appropriate boat shoes like a good girl, grippy soles and covered toes but have been struggling with the most ridiculous two tone feet. The edge of my feet and toes are lily white (my usual colour year round actually) and the inner top part of my feet and ankles up, now I'm a member of the outdoors brigade is a caramel colour. I finally got sick of it today and as we had no locks thought I'd bare feet to try and match them up a bit, after comments of inappropriate footwear from him and some eye rolling from me. I flip flopped off down the gunnel (the sticky out bit on the side where sensible shoes are advised). Yes, the inevitable happened, caught the flip flop in the gap in the gunnel and off it pinged with an audible 'ploink' straight into the water. They may have only been a fiver but I liked them and needed both to be able to continue using them for their intended purpose. So brandishing the big hooky stick thing, I made the puffed up Mr know it all reverse back on a salvage shoe mission. As I write this the flip flop is drying on the roof and I've decided to go bare foot. I will not be told.

We have found a beautiful place to moor up, only sheep and ducks for company and they are on the far bank so personal space has been respected by all parties. It is so nice here I may hide the boat keys so we stay forever. As Mr Fedex seems on such a mission to move, move, move it'll do him some good to do some fishing or paint the landscape.

After dinner we decided to have a fire, not setting alight the woods or anything but on the towpath campfire style. Deadwood, kindling and suitable tinder were dutifully collected ready for our fire barrel. I, yes I lit the fire, now that may not sound very impressive, shove your zippo on it and away you go, but no, this fire was started with no matches or lighter and certainly no lighter fluid. I made actual real fire with only a flint stick and my own awesomeness! It felt incredible, never before had I attempted to start a fire with just two bits of metal, the sparks they created and my slightly wine tinged breath. I'll admit it got a bit tense, with Captain 'here let me show you' and 'first mate 'no get away I can do it' staring each other out, but when I told him to shag off and get me some more tinder, things settled down and I got on with my cavewoman thing. I only bloody did it, I made fire! I felt like Tom Hanks in Castaway, granted our requirement for fire was only romance and adventure, whereas Tom's life sort of depended on it and again, granted we had array of fire lighting paraphernalia on board should I have got cross with the flint stick and Tom only had wood, but still, I leapt about shouting 'I made fire, I am the greatest.

Travelling - Between bridge 8w and 9w - to - Nowhere
Date - 03/09/14

The ducks here are either stupid, shy or victims of bullying. Usually as soon as you are moored up ducks swim over to see if you're giving away any tasty titbits and if you dare to rustle a bread bag they literally take to the air to get to your boat quicker. This brace of ducks, not even close, even when I've thrown bread in the water only 3 of the group showed an interest, but they only manage to swim halfway before looking bored, turning around and going back to its buddies, very odd.

Being this close to nature I can tell you that sheep sound like they are slurping up water rather than lapping at it when drinking out of the canal, that they waggle their tails around to get rid of poo and that sometimes they make a gross dry heaving sound. What I can't tell you is why so many sheep have bad legs? In every field we have passed there have been one or two limping sheep. In this field I'm sat opposite, there are loads of limpers, what's that all about? Do they fake an injury so as not to become the next mutton stew, are cattle generally prone arthritis or do they get stones in their hooves? They look plump and content so I don't think this hobbling is neglect but whatever it is, it certainly seems common.

Well that is just peculiar, when we moored up between bridges 8 and 9 we did it because it was isolated, not a soul in sight apart from, of course the sheep and ducks but at 4 O'clock today, instead of passing us with a wave like every other boat has done, this boat moors up, now I cannot claim to own the territory but did it really need to moor up so close to Billow that it used the same metal mooring ring as us? That is just odd, if you were desperate for the fantastic view just moor up two or three rings along, we don't need to be touching! There is no one else here to squash us nose to tail you weirdos, you've made me feel uncomfortable, would you sit next to me on an empty train too. Of course Roly got chatting to them, that man will talk to anyone.

Travelling - Bridge 8 - 9 - to - Somewhere else
Date - 01/09/14

We are moving on today and I shall be keeping my eye out for the boat I have christened 'No Personal Space' in case it follows us. Not sure how we will give it the slip if it does as we travel at walking pace and just go in one direction. A disguise perhaps, a moustache for Roly and a blonde wig for me, maybe a Thomas the tank engine costume for the boat.

Why am I seeing different animals in different parts of the country? Before 9am this morning we saw three grey squirrels, they were all heading in the same direction so they may have been heading to a function but why different creatures in different parts, apart from the cattle and waterfowl obviously.

All along the canal people have had stuff to sell, we've bought fruit, veg, preserves and even meat from a farm and of course eggs. Today though I watched a man whose house was on a lock, well next to it, with goods on a stall set out on his garden wall suitable for any good jumble sale. He had tea cups and spoons, books and clothes. He fussed around it like an ant looking after the queens young. Picking bits up, wiping them clean, moving a cup here, a book there. I daren't go and have a nose at his wares in case he thought I was some sort of threat and attacked me.

We are now in Wales, I know this because a sign welcomed me before we had to circumnavigate a tunnel. A very tight narrow tunnel, made more difficult by the current. Normally a canal doesn't have a current but the Llangollen canal is fed by water from the horseshoe falls on its way to a reservoir somewhere (disclaimer: I do not know this to be true. I have just been told that and chose to go with it). This current means that if you floor it to achieve maximum speed, a whole six miles an hour, you will be lucky if you get three. We spent the first few hours on this canal thinking something was wrong with the boat, Roly must have checked the propeller for debris half a dozen times. At least on the way back we will be going with the current, although doubt we will be close to breaking the water speed record. So this tunnel, is 421 metres long, has a 2.08 metre beam and a 2.29 metre air draft. Now I know what metres are, but the rest, not a clue. all I know is, that tunnel was tight and Roly who gets a bit twitchy in tight spaces emerged blinking into the light looking like he had been on a white knuckle ride, lots of sugary tea and heaps of praise helped calm his nerves.

Travelling - Chrich - to - The aqueduct
Date - 05/09/14

Today could be the day! We came on this canal to 'do' the Pontcysyllte aqueduct and we are nearly there, depending on which information you chose to believe the water bridge is either 135 or 120 foot high. I am so excited, Roly however, after his unnerving tunnel experience is crapping his pants (although I'm not supposed to tell you that).

Change of plan, we stopped for a pub lunch, again yes I know. We will need rolling out of this boat soon. After consuming our grub, we went for a walk and I spotted a sign for an auction viewing so we went for a gander. Of course I, like a magpie spotted some bits that sparkled and having never been to an auction plus discovering the event was tomorrow decided we are hanging around Froncysyllte so we could get involved, who needs a massive water bridge when jewellery is up for grabs!

We walked across the aqueduct just to take in the views, beautiful obviously, we are in Wales after all. Roly held the handrail all the way across bless him but hats off, he did it.

Travelling - Froncysyllte - to - Nowhere
Date - 06/09/14

Auction day. I was very excited, I pondered over my cereal what it would be like, is it really like those cash in the attic type programs. Turns out, yes it was. I wanted to bid on everything, partly because I wanted to lift my bid card up and have a serious dealer/collector face on, just so people thought 'ohhh she knows what she's doing' but also because I kept thinking, bet that will be worth something when I'm dead.

So I went with the intention of bidding on one of the two rings that caught my eye in the viewing, but I came away with 5 items, I thought that only happened when I went to supermarkets. I got the two rings, for a bargain price I might add, so having both was ok, promise. I also bought a silver charm bracelet from the '70's, no idea why I bought that, it just reminded me of my childhood, I had one when I was young and added charms from places I visited. Not sure what I'm going to do with it, maybe nostalgia made me buy it, but even now I'm staring at it with a confused look on my face asking myself why? The other two items were far more sensible. I bought a camera from the 1920's for my brother for Christmas, he is into that stuff and if he doesn't like it he can flog it on. Lastly, my obsession with a bargain lead me to buy a set of 8 hardback books covering the fall of the Roman Empire. Quite honestly that isn't a subject that interests me, however the fact they were printed in 1855 and the fact the auctioneers estimate on them was £100-£150 did interest me, especially when no one else wanted them. I got those bad boys for just £30!! One of two things will happen with those glorious old books, either Roly will finally build me the library he knows I desperately want and they will be housed in a special 'look at my fancy books' section, away from Stephen King in the 'more interesting reading' section or they will be carefully wrapped up in protective clothing and stored in the attic (when I have an attic once again) to be carried down and taken to the grandkids equivalent of Antiques Roadshow when I'm well past it and they want some cash. £30 for 8 hardback books in immaculate condition that are nearly 160 years old, serious bargain to me, and they did not see me coming at all!

Travelling - Froncysyllte - to - Llangollen
Date - 07/09/14

Today was aqueduct day. Before we got there we needed to fill up with water and, as I was holding the centre rope I saw a tiny bat continuously flying around in a big circle between the trees. I watched it dance its frantic dance for a while wondering why such a tiny bat was flapping around at 9am in bright sunlight. Roly decided that he, if indeed the creature was a male, had been on an all-night bender and this was his flight of shame home. As he was only flying in a circle I had him down as a baby that had gotten lost. I wanted to catch him, wrap him up in a blanket and put him in a box until nighttime before letting him out at dusk to be reunited with his family. Right now he stuck out like a very tiny sore thumb, breakfast for any nimble bird of prey. Did the stupid bat not know he was on the protected list? As I didn't have a net or a partner who cared enough to quickly fashion a net out of his boxer shorts and a stick I could only watch helplessly, sending him telepathic messages to hide until dark.

Aqueduct done, stunning views, amazing height and one very brave Roly. He even managed to take a photo or two.

The Llangollen is the busiest canal, I don't know if that's in the UK, the world or the universe but it is easy to see why, the scenery is absolutely stunning! The water is clear, or that could just be the fact it is so shallow. The only downside was, indeed the volume of traffic, it seems there are hundreds of holiday hire boats about. We assumed it would have quieted down the first week of September, but no, the waters are still full of them. Hire boats aren't our favorite thing, they never slow down for moored boats, causing you to rock about all over the place and passing them can be tricky as they try to work out their arse from the elbow. I am sure a very high percentage are

50

more than competent so I apologise for tarring you all with the same brush, how quickly I've become an opinionated know it all!

Travelling - Llangollen - to - Staying put
Date - 08/09/14

The last bit of the canal at Llangollen is so narrow it, like the aqueduct is single file, one at a time and if you moor up for more than 4hrs you have to pay to park, (although that did give you an electricity point). I, being the spotter for the day had walked ahead to check the coast, or in this case, canal was clear of oncoming traffic, but witnessed the arse end of bedlam with at least 10 boats ahead waiting to get through. I dutifully reported back to the captain any attempt to move would be futile and we may as well stay put until things calmed down, it was lunchtime after all. We moored up, walked into town and had some lunch. Every boat we passed heading into the town was a hire boat, Roly's favorite. That should be fun later. After lunch and a bit of Christmas shopping, we headed back to the boat and tried again to get Billow closer to town, I ambled ahead and spotting a vacant space and no oncoming boats I phoned Roly to say all clear ahead, get moving now. As he slowly made his way towards the spot I fiercely guarding I wondered how they did this before mobiles. A lot of running and hand signals I imagine.

Moored up and with no need to head back into town, parking fee paid, toilet emptied and electric plugged in we sat back and watched the comedy show that was narrow boats trying to pass each other on a single width canal. The entertainment was well worth the mooring fee. Most hadn't sent someone ahead to actually check they could get through and those that had been sensible enough to send a spotter had chosen to use imbeciles, morons that didn't understand the concept of one boat in one direction at a time. all afternoon we enjoyed ourselves watching canal chaos. Boats meeting head on, lots of swearing and men blaming everything around them. Like an animal fight in the wild the weaker boater having to concede and reverse back the way he came, trying to remain straight but usually veering off at all sorts of strange angles, with members of his party helpfully shouting useless instructions, their voices raising in sheer panic, only for the hapless reverser to then meet another boat that had decided to set forth without looking ahead, so now two boats of the hired variety were reversing to make way for the more dominant male. We had hours of fun watching this spectacle, with multitudes of boats trying to arrive or leave.

We had decided tonight was bath/hotel night and for a change we decided to have a night off from each other, of course I got the hotel. Don't get me wrong, a night off did not mean we were ready to call it a day and come home. No, we were still enjoying it and each other, of course there were moments we wanted to strangle each other, or at least accidentally push the other into the canal but on the whole we were loving it. It is just that prior to this trip Roly and I had never spent so much time together, hell we didn't even live together, nearly ten years together and we still lived in different houses. Hey it works for us! So 6 weeks on a 57ft narrowboat being together 24/7 and I do mean 24/7 was a cause for celebration and we will do it being spending the night apart.

Travelling - Llangollen - to - Not moving
Date - 09/09/14

I write this from my hotel room, last night's bath lasted two hours and one whole bottle of wine. That is what I call a bath, it was wonderfully deep, I could have easily gotten lost in it. I have now decided there needs to be a regulation on bath depths, too shallow and a person in a suit carrying a clip board will tut at you, this tutty bath inspector has the power to remove your hotel licence or something. Maybe I could apply for the role, chief bath tester. Anyway the soak was divine and the bed was so soft I woke up in the night convinced I was being eaten by a marshmallow, quite scary. I didn't sleep well without Roly next to me but don't tell him that!

Travelling - Llangollen - to - Backwards
Date - 10/09/14

Time to leave today. Llangollen was as lovely as ever and I recommend everyone to visit, just not at the same time please, you'll spoil it. I stocked up on a few presents for Christmas, my work here is done. Back over that aqueduct and through the tunnel, then another tunnel and finally another, albeit little aqueduct and then we are once again in England. We have to head back the way we came as the Llangollen canal just ends. Think we will head south next, we shall see. Unlike Frodo Baggins we have no quest so can nonchalantly turn left or right whenever a junction appears.

Travelling - Somewhere - to - Somewhere else
Date - 11/09/14

I had to hide in the boat for a bit today, I couldn't contain my laughter so had to make myself scarce, until I had grown up into an adult instead of a giggling child. We came upon a traffic jam, a barrage of holiday hire boats queuing for the water point and lock, incidentally this was the lock with the weird jumble sale wall man. The reason for my chuckling was because everyone had got involved with 'helping' and were so busy barking instructions at each other, no one really had a clue what was happening. There was one particularly loud guy, British, who had seemingly designated himself leader and kept walking up and down the tow path full of people holding their centre ropes. Telling them who precisely was doing what and when they were doing it. Well the Americans and the Australians did as they were told, but the Brits wanted it do it themselves and were arguing back. Then there were those without hire boats, who just got on with it, us included, ignoring the Sargent Major. We didn't need water, just passage through, so onwards we headed, leaving the self-appointed captain to it. Oddly, or perhaps not, the only people helping at the actual lock, were live aboards or permanent owners, we all exchanged comical raised eyebrows at the farce behind us whilst trying to avoid the strange man touching his wares on the wall. I am now officially a full of myself boat snob. I couldn't help it, the hire boaters didn't ask for my disdain but it is just like watching the chuckle brothers on water. I am either laughing or rolling eyes, someone really needs to put me in my place.

Travelling - Along the canal - to - Ellesmere
Date - 12/09/14

Yes, I finally found it, my journey is complete my adventure over! Okay, that is a bit extreme but I did find my holy grail. We timed our return trip to co-inside with the Ellesmere floating market, hoping it would be an improvement on the last one and there, in all its glory was. . . . The Cheese Boat, I feel complete and will of course be eating cheese with everything for the next month. I almost skipped over to the boat waving my purse at the owner, whilst demurely fluttering my eyelids going cooee! No other words needed today, content Jayne.

Travelling - Still Ellesmere - to - Same place
Date - 13/09/14

I appreciate that by sitting on the tow path doing my jigsaw, I am inviting witty one-liners and questions galore. Add in Roly fishing, cross legged on top of the boat like a gnome, plus the busy floating market visitors and today we have been inundated with people stopping to chat. Being canal folk I've had to become more social, at home I had no reason to hold idle chats and smiley conversations with strangers, I imagine mainly, because I didn't just sit in the street reading or doing puzzles. On the boat though, it is expected. Everyone, even me to a degree is friendly and they want to talk, except me, mostly I don't want to talk but as I say, by sitting canalside I have to get involved else I shall forever be remembered as that ignorant bitch on Billow. So ready with answers to 'oh have you been doing that long?', 'is it a hard puzzle?' Incidentally with my current jigsaw the answer is very much YES, it is ridiculously hard. We also got 'have you caught anything', which I am assuming is aimed at Roly rather than a personal question to me about diseases. Then there is 'do you live on your boat', 'where are you heading' and 'do you wanna buy a daaawg' - No I made that last one up, well stole it from a film actually. A lady asked 'Why is she called Billow'. We don't know, we bought her already named, but the lady hangs around still chatting. She was sharing nice canal routes with Roly and talking about her boat. Pleasant lady, widowed young grandmother sort, she did tell us her marital status, I didn't just decide on her back story as I tried to look busy on my jigsaw. She then started talking about canal boat forums with advice and routes etc, not really our thing but we nod and smile politely, then is gets weird, not sinister (although that would be a more interesting tale), this sweet granny starts telling me quietly about a special chat room for women on the canals, women only mind. Not only is it women only, it is secret and you won't find it on google I am told, then she gives me a conspiring look and says you can only join when another lady invites you. what the Frock?! Why do they need a secret protected site, why no men, if I join will I have to sacrifice a man or boy or something? The young granny then reassures me absolutely no men and as it is invite only men can't pretend to be women and join, phew that's a relief! I wondered as she went on 'selling' it to me if these desperate to join men went, so far as to dress up as women trying to befriend ladies just to gain access to this allusive site. If you are wondering why the strict no males policy, ready for this. . . . it's because they don't want men talking about engines and stuff. I say again, what the actual frock, except of course my mind uses the actual profanity. So when I ask what is it for, this anti men secret on line haven, she divulges, that at the moment a lady's dog is dying and they are all offering support. To re-cap, as I have waffled on a bit, this is a top secret anti-man forum for women to discuss death, maybe sinister is closer to the truth. I dare not look in case I am pulled into this cult!

Oh yes, revenge sweet revenge. I finally have payback for Roly's endless laughing about my car park ticket faux pas. In Tesco, at the tobacconists and Roly confidentially asks for 50 grams of Golden Vagina. Both the assistant and I were laughing so hard we had to hold onto the counter to prevent total collapse, Roly turned a lovely shade of pink. To add the cherry to the already beautifully iced cake, the guy calls over one of his colleagues to tell him what happened right in front of the already dying Roly. I am going to dine on that for weeks.

Travelling - Ellesmere - to - Here still
Date - 15/09/14

I had been toying with the idea of getting Roly a chainsaw for Christmas, I had even called upon my tree surgeon cousin for brand recommendations and had research them secretly on line, when Roly announces last night over dinner that he needs a chainsaw in his life. Well, funny you should say that dear, as I showed him the models I'd been looking at The look of love on his face because he was getting one was very moving, or maybe it was actually aimed at the tools we were perusing. After realising this needed to be an early Christmas present, we went chainsaw shopping today. Nothing in Ellesmere but several helpful shop keepers pointed us in the direction of an industrial estate in Oswestry, which, as we were carless would involve buses, this would be interesting.

After securing a bus number, a bus timetable and directions to the estate off we strode, me with a determined walk and Roly like a kid on his way to see Santa. Thankfully using a bus hasn't changed since I was a child, you stand at the stop, hand the driver your money and receive a ticket, then, the best part, ding the bell when you get to your required destination. What felt like it had changed, but surely was only our imagination, was the speed. After being on a narrow boat doing walking speed, this public transport vehicle felt like it was doing warp speed, I can't remember the last time scenery moved so fast. Two bus rides and a two mile round trip walk and Roly is now the proud owner of a shiny new Stihl, sure he was cuddling it on the bus home.

We decided, as we are in the area we would do the Montgomery canal. Because it's a canal in the process of being restored the locks for entry are only in use between 12 and 2 daily, so you need to pre book your slot, no mean feat in an area neither of us can get signal. So we climbed tall buildings and stretched ourselves to the point of mobile reception and then had to leave messages anyway, both of us did. I then pulled the short straw, staying around to maintain 1 bar of coverage until the Canal & River Trust called back, thankfully they didn't leave me hanging allowed too long. Slot all booked for tomorrow.

Travelling - The edge of Montgomery - to - Montgomery canal
Date - 16/09/14

I did my first winding hole today, as the queue to get onto the Montgomery locks were all on one side we had to go along a bit and then turn the boat around. A winding hole is an extra bit cut into the canal for boats to turn in. we pronounce it winding, as in wind her up, some pronounce it as in blowing a gale. I have no idea which is correct and whenever I ask I am told either. I am pleased to report I turned all 57foot 3 inches of boat around in a 70foot hole, with no drama. I didn't hit anything, I didn't sink anything and I didn't shout at Roly for telling me what to do. I cannot claim to have completed the manoeuvre as a 3-point turn, but complete it in less than 20 I did!

As the locks at the entrance to the Montgomery having opening times we thought we would head in at 12:30 then stop for a bit of lunch. Who were we kidding, it was like a very slow version of Piccadilly Circus with boats going in and out. We did finally get through the four locks and break for lunch at 2:30.

It has been a week since we were last at a pub, better for the waistline, cholesterol and wallet but I had certainly missed the interesting things you see. Take this woman for instance.

Across the way from us as we are eating our tea and enjoying a nice glass of red were a couple having a drink and sharing a bag of peanuts, she did, in my opinion eat them oddly. Now I'm not saying she should have just poured the whole bag of nuts down her throat but she ate 1 peanut at a time and methodically chewed it, I mean really really slowly. I too have a slight OCD with peanuts, I have to eat the half ones first, saving the whole ones for last, but at least I still chuck a handful in once I've done my weird sorting out. I reckon, if left to her own devices that peanut eater could have made that bag last for hours. I have chewed tough badly cooked meat quicker than that.

Travelling - Montgomery - to - And back
Date - 17/09/14

The latter part of the Montgomery canal is not for the fainthearted, you can hear the underside of the boat scraping along the bottom and the flora is fighting a turf war with the recently restored canal for ownership rights. The plants want the canal back and will seemingly do anything in their power to get it back. I feel I should be wearing old fashioned safari garb, including hat of course, whilst standing at the front of the boat brandishing a machete to cut a way through the bush.

The Montgomery was short but lovely and on leaving I watched a man blackberrying, I'm still trying to work out if he was cheating or using his initiative. He was using long handled shears, hacking off bunches, selecting the good ripe ones and throwing the rest. Was that wasteful and selfish or was that resourceful. One thing I do know is, I have never seen such an abundance of blackberries, our whole journey, we have been surrounded by them. It's a shame I don't really like them much anymore, maybe a childhood overdose, because they could have fed us forever.

Travelling - Along the way a bit
Date - 18/09/14

Roly got to use his chainsaw today. We finally stopped purely to sort out the growing pile of wood on the roof, he no doubt got sick of my moaning about how messy it was. I don't want to become one of those ugly live aboard boats that have as much stuff on top, as they likely have inside. Our winter log stock pile was growing well. Even I have been foraging for bits of broken dead tree. So he chain sawed the big bits and I hand sawed the smaller bits. I did have a go on the new toy, loved the noise, power and skills, just didn't like the thought of hacking my leg off. We now have a nice neat pile of symmetrical logs all hidden away in the cratch, that's the bit at the front of the boat, not a misspelling.

I am getting more than a bit frustrated with the kingfishers. Why, oh why can't they hold still for just two seconds. I want to see them in all their glory and get a sneaky photo. All we do get is a flash of dazzling blue and they are gone. If one could just sit still on a branch, perhaps offer up a regal pose, I could die happy.

We spotted a chestnut tree today and not being ones to miss an opportunity, I hopped off the boat to collect some.

Travelling - Grindley Brook - to - Someplace else
Date - 19/09/14

Late last night Roly was leaning out of the side doors having a smoke when he shouts 'quick, Jayne come and look' So I scramble over to join him and peer into the inky blackness of the autumn night. 'What I don't see anything', Roly grabs a flashlight and points it across the water, 'I saw an otter' unless this otter was wearing a hi-vis jacket I'm not convinced 'are you sure, it is very dark out here' I ask whilst trying to keep the disbelief out of my voice. I leave him to it and return to the sofa, a few minutes later he joins me and as he plonks himself down he says 'actually I think it was a squirrel, yeah now I think about it, it had a bushy tail' ??!! I leapt up 'was it drowning', all prepared to whip off my jim jams and dive in after it. 'No he declares, 'it dived in one side, swam across and climbed out the other side'. What? Now I know he is not drunk so I better check the mushrooms to see if we picked up the hallucinogenic kind in error. Strange episode, odd man.

I absolutely swear what I am about to write is true, a massive co-incidence after what I wrote this morning but 100% true none the less and if you don't believe me you can ask my sister as I was on the phone to her as it happened. Here it is, I was walking along the towpath towards the lock bridge we had to negotiate, catching up with my sis on the phone, you already knew that bit. When out of the bushes dashes a grey squirrel, he obviously thought he had the area to himself so was startled when he saw me swinging my windlass and gassing on a mobile, so startled in fact that he launched himself into the canal, shock clearly preventing him from sensibly going back the way he came. Up into the air he jumped and landed with a splash, I don't know who was more surprised him or me. With

61

a pause in family catch up to deliver breaking animal news as it happened, live, I lean to the edge of the water, wondering if I would see him do the breast stroke. No, as suspected, the poor wet rodent was desperately trying to clamber out, without much success initially. Whilst trying to work out how I could use my windlass to hoik him out, so I didn't have to use my own vulnerable hand and get bitten, he managed to grab some overhanging weeds and pull himself out. He shot back into the bushes like his arse was on fire. I pointed out his obvious unhappiness at being in the canal to Roly later and his reply was 'so, some mammals don't like water, doesn't mean we all are the same', nope can't argue with that and yes squirrels can swim, google told me.

Travelling - Hurleston locks - to - Left, not right
Date - 20/09/14

As we were approaching Hurleston locks we were still undecided on which way to go when we got to the bottom, left to Chester or right to Wolverhampton, then it occurred to me. When do we ever get to make such last minute carefree decisions? In 'real' life, even if the weekend is your own, you don't tend to wing it to such a degree, well we never did. I'm a planner, an organiser, I get agitated if I don't know what is happening next. I freak out if I'm late for anything and if I'm not in control, woe betide the world. Yet here I am, at the top of the lock staircase shrugging my shoulders and saying 'I don't mind, let's toss a coin'. My own family wouldn't have recognised me, hell I had to look behind me to see who spoke.

The decider was the zoo, we are heading to Chester to visit the zoo. Last time I was there they had an orangutan with hair so long he had dreadlocks, what more do you need.

Travelling - Hargrave - to - This way a bit
Date - 21/09/14

Interesting night's sleep had! Just before we moored up for the day yesterday we passed a couple of boats doubled up so they were side by side instead of nose to tail, they had a private mooring with a little bit of land. On their 'patch' were a few crates of beer and a homemade pizza oven. It looked like a group of people having a bit of a lovely get together at 3 in the afternoon. The name of the boat should have set alarm bells ringing, if you live aboard a boat called Sesh, you clearly named it that for a reason. We moored up a reasonable distance away, maybe 350 metres and on the towpath side, the opposite side to Sesh. Roly claims to have heard them all night, but as he sleeps like the dead that seems unlikely. I didn't hear a thing . . . until 4am, when we were rudely awakened, heart in your mouth, where's the baddy style by two men swearing and shouting walking past the boat, that was then followed by a boat full of more drunk sweary people, at least they had put the headlight on, safety first people.

What a set of locks! The 32ft, three lock staircase in Chester was immense. Unfortunately, the top two, as we were going down, only had one paddle. Why would you have double width (big enough for two boats) locks with only one opening for the water? They took so long to fill I could have had a nap, meanwhile Roly is topside, keeping an audience as he nonchalantly leans on the lock waiting for it to empty. By the time we got to the bottom lock I was the prize specimen in a rather grubby glassless aquarium, there must have been about 30 people watching and one woman took so many photos of me and Billow that we both started getting a complex and I considered charging her. On the plus side, we have a new pet. As the water went down in the first lock I noticed the wall was covered in tiny mollusc's, they squirted water as they closed. I was fascinated, as I had never seen a mussel in a lock before, other half aside of course. The lock was too deep for me to show Roly, so in the name of learning, well sort of, I pulled one off the wall so I could show him. As previously mentioned, the lock took an age and guilt started to set in, there sitting on the roof of my boat was a tiny thumbnail sized creature, probably wondering why he or she had been torn from the space picked to live upon. The only thing to do was throw away the rest of Roly's cider (well I was drinking mine and he had less left) and collect some canal water for the relocated shellfish. When we got to the bottom, something like four days later, I waved this murky glass at Roly and said look at this, I had to empty the glass so he could actually see the treasure. Research tells me he is a zebra mussel, originally from Russia, accidentally released here and other places around the world. Not sure how you 'accidentally' introduce a new species, did they fall out of someone's collecting box as a stroll was taken one day? Anyway, I've decided to keep him for a bit. I have created a little haven for Marty, named after the zebra in Madagascar obviously. I say haven, I mean tupperware filled with canal water and stone Roly had collected. He looks content and I'm engrossed watching him move about.

Travelling - Chester - to - The zoo
Date - 22/09/14

After changing Marty's water to 'clean' dirty canal water and assuring him we would be back later we headed off to the zoo. I love a zoo and we spent hours traipsing round looking and reading about everything. Did you know elephants have 100,00 muscles just in theirs trunks and they don't like chilies? Also the Javan green magpie is the most endangered bird in the world (that was in 2014, please don't get in touch if there are

64

none left, I still mourn lonesome George) and just one drop of poison from the golden poison frog is enough to kill 20 men, bet volunteer 21 was relieved when they were doing that test. Included in our ticket price were two exhibits not mentioned on the map. The first, a fearless field mouse running around in the chimpanzee house, our side of the glass not theirs. He was certainly no Mr Jingles but we all stopped starring at the chimps to watch this tiny round bodied rodent scurry about on the floor, well we can see the primates every day if we so wish, but who is lucky enough to see a mouse visiting the zoo. The second was really just a performance of begging but unlike Mr Bumble, we were enchanted and happily gave more, half our sandwiches actually to the collection of sparrows and starlings that had joined us at our picnic table. The sparrows being much smaller and wearing much less dazzling plumage than the beautiful starlings had to up their game to ensure they didn't miss out, so they were brave enough to take bread from our fingers. The starlings however, just stood on the table waiting for us to throw bits of sandwich in their direction. Neither of these two added bonuses outshone the collection of animals Chester had to offer, nor did they distract from all the conservation information Chester wanted us to understand, but I loved them nonetheless. My feet are now killing me, 5hours at the zoo, plus the walk there & back means a foot soak & feet up for us tonight, we will have to argue over who is getting up to pour the wine later.

Travelling - Chester - to - Back the way we came
Date - 23/09/14

We thought we would stay on the Shropshire canal until we came to the end at Ellesmere Port, but the further along we went the more industrial it became. Not what we are interested in seeing, nothing against grey concrete and razor wire I just don't find it as aesthetically pleasing as the autumn leaves trying to outdo each other with their vivid colours and the wildlife doing its own thing every day. If your one of those that likes to go for a drive, usually on a Sunday, you head to the country not to an industrial estate, same principle on a boat.

Travelling - Bunbury - to - Middlewich branch
Date - 25/09/14

I thought after two months I was lock fit. Bingo wings toned lower back and leg muscles primed to handle anything and then we entered the Middlewich branch of the Shropshire Union and man was I wrong. The last two locks we have done were ridiculous, I literally had to jump on the paddles to get them turning and because there were so many boats ahead of us I did the first lock three times. The second lock, after discovering it was even harder than the first, I did once then strolled back to the boat and informed Roly, 'actually it's my turn to drive now'. What grates me a little is people that don't get stuck in. Without wanting to sound too much like Roly, a lot of the hire boaters all stand around until it's their turn. No, get your butt and your shiny windlass up to the lock, if there is always four people working the lock the process is much quicker, plus I won't feel bitter about helping you if you have helped too.

Travelling - Church Minsull - to - A bit closer
Date - 26/09/14

I met a lovely young man and his dad at big lock in Middlewich. The lad was in a wheelchair and I'll be honest I couldn't understand him well but his dad talked me through the gist. Apparently, his newest hobby was locks, not even necessarily the boats. His dad had got him a windlass and they had driven from North Wales to Middlewich so the boy could do some locks, I say boy but I'm rubbish at the age guessing game so he could have been anything from 14 to 24. He got stuck in with doing the paddle for me and helped open the gate but the best bit as far as I'm concerned was him instructing Roly that it was his turn to leave the lock, anyone that can tell Roly what to do is alright in my book. I even stayed behind to help him do the lock for the next boat, in fact I could have stayed all day I was having such a good time and his enjoyment was infectious but Roly was at the bottom hanging onto the boat wondering where I had got too.

On our way to the Anderton bridge we saw a little picnic area, not on the towpath side the other side. It was just for boaters, as there appeared to be no access on foot. There are a couple of picnic tables, with BBQ stands next to them and then just woods and water. It is so peaceful I think we may stay a while. I could do with the wind dropping a bit then I could whip out a jigsaw, yep hardcore I know. Instead, for now I shall have an explore and then a read, it will shortly be wine o'clock after all.

Travelling - Bramble Cuttings - to - A bit further
Date - 27/09/14

That little isolated area was lovely, there was lots of dead wood for Roly to play with as I got lost in a book. We fashioned a washing line and got some washing out to dry. We ate and drank at 'our' bench, feeling like we were miles away from civilisation, it was bliss. As an added feature a nearby fudge boat was in full production mode and the air was thick with the sweet heady smell of melting sugar, it was enough to make you want to gnaw your own arm off. Roly was duly dispatched to go and buy some as I, over the years have grown attached to both arms. That fudge was bloody gorgeous.

All good things must come to an end and despite wanting to stay another night we can't, we are almost out of water. I did consider asking Roly swim to the next water point and collect some in a container, but it might be a bit far and, don't tell him, but I'd probably miss him. Therefore, sadly we must leave, we have made a promise to stay again on the way back.

Travelling - Anderton boat lift - to - River Weaver
Date - 28/09/14

We moored up to book a slot on the Anderton and whilst we were waiting and had finished our chores, we went to watch the lift bridge in action. I say action, using the word loosely. Not a lot happened on the outside, a bit of noise then the lifts swapped places, one going up and one going down then boats came out. I was hoping being inside would be a little more exciting. It is something to do with two hydraulics and using the water. One bit pushes up forcing the other down vertically 50ft between the River Weaver and the Trent & Mersey. Now it is operated with electrics, it looked fascinating anyway even if I didn't know or care about the mechanics. Clearly many people do, the place was busy with tourists, not even on boats!

Two boats go in one lift and we shared with a boat called Penguin, sounded quirky, I can work with that. Whilst waiting to be 'safety briefed' we met the occupants of Penguin, he had long white hair and they looked like a proper canal couple. Oddly, I wanted to sniff him as I suspected he would smell of engines and must, a bit like my Uncle Jack, but I thought they may think me rude so I refrained. After excitedly telling him this was our first time, he told me he first did it in '72 with Charlie Atkins, politely I smiled and nodded wondering if I was supposed to know who that was, he then asked me if I knew who Charlie was, 'no' I admitted, he replied 'shame' but then didn't go on to enlighten me. (According to Google Charlie Atkins had one of the last working boats, so now I know if asked again). This weathered white haired man then proceeded to tell me his boat bottom was 100yrs old (why just the bottom)? And that it was a wind up (boat, not as in stitch up I assume, as he was quite into giving me the talk). Also he said something remarkably like Bollinger, but sadly I know he wasn't referring to the bubbly just something on his boat that sounds like Bollinger but isn't. Thankfully, at that moment, just before I yawned or sniffed him, our attendant arrived to talk to us about the all-important health and safety, because obviously as morons it was likely without proper instruction we would fall off the lift to our deaths 50ft below. So, do not walk on the gunnel, do not walk on the roof etc. Suitably educated on surviving we were permitted to enter the lift with Penguin alongside. This time thankfully Roly got chatting to him about engines and old stuff.

Bits closed, clunked and filled with water and the world's slowest theme park ride got started, it was never going to make us throw our arms up screaming or launch our stomachs into our mouths but even in its slowness I enjoyed the descent. Amazing that it was constructed in 1875.

Travelling - River Weaver - to - Bramble Cutting
Date - 29/09/14

Back up the lift today, as we didn't fancy staying on the river, nothing against it, I'm sure had we chosen to navigate it we would have enjoyed the trip but we were really missing our lovely little spot called Brambles cuttings. What we did see of the Weaver was pleasant and there was a Waitrose , always good for a fake snob like me. The only thing that let it down was two new additions to the river, I assume they had only recently been added as their contents were still floating lazily about on the water. Some thoughtful person or persons had added, for whose benefit I'm not sure, two large full commercial bins. Biffa will be pleased with the advertising I'm sure.

Travelling - Bramble Cutting - to - Away from there
Date - 01/10/14

You mate, are not what I need today. Wind your awful know it all neck in before I rip you to pieces with my caustic tongue and, if I do say so myself, my deadly dirty look. Today is not a good day.

Yesterday my daughter had to have the cat put down, our black and white, annoyingly long haired fur ball. He who shed fur on everything, only came over for a fuss if he wanted something or you were male and he, oh he that knew it was time for the groomers before I had even got the cat carrier down and would think of more and more elaborate ways of escape. He didn't go to the groomers for a cut and colour, or to have policy painted on his nails, no Sebastian went to the groomers for a simple comb. Where it took four of them to actually brush him. I had given up trying to do it myself years ago, for it was a battle I always lost and the only bloodshed was of course mine. Many a time I had threatened to have him waxed all over. I am sad that he had to be put down, but what I feel the most is guilt, I wish Chloe hadn't had to do it, I should have been there. Lots of tears for both cat and baby girl, so brave.

So back to my earlier comments, that means I do not need some know it all anorak, telling me which paddle I should open first or which side Roly should tie up on. You get to come down when we have finished coming up, so either get stuck in and help or go back to rubbing the leather on your windlass pouch. We have our system and it most definitely does not involve canal nerds wearing leather telling us what to do. Yes he actually did have strapped to him, a nice shiny new leather belt with a special pouch for a windlass, nope never seen one of those before.

Travelling - Wheelock - to - Someplace else
Date - 02/10/14

We woke up to our first real autumnal morning today. Mist rolling along the top of the water, fog on your breath and condensation on every porthole! First job of the day, dry all the windows. I have a feeling that will be the case every morning now, oh well, small price to pay for such a stunning view. It was the first time I had to wear gloves to operate the locks today, they were bloody freezing, but by lunchtime, we had stripped off to our t-shirts again. The beginning of October and we are warm enough for short sleeves, I think we have been very lucky so far and just to clarify, it isn't t-shirts alone we are parading about in, we are wearing jeans too and the obligatory boat gypsy headscarf for me.

Lots of locks today and most are duplicated, which just means two locks side by side. Not sure why Thomas Telford thought this bit of the Trent and Mersey canal needed 25 locks turning into 50, perhaps the working boat traffic was bad round here back in the day. We are going up, which I have just decided is more interesting than going down as least when it's my turn to drive. You don't know what you'll see when your head and boat slowly pop up, meerkat style. A field of cows, a row of houses, acres of swaying sweetcorn whispering 'come and scrump us' or a field of hobbling wool covered sheep. Although usually you can smell the cattle way before you rise up to see them. I am getting good at identifying which animals we are approaching by the smell of the poo, I know, who would have thought it. It's not really a skill that is going to get me far or impress people but there you have it, I am now a shit sniffer.

Travelling - Church Lawton - to - Stoke on Trent
Date - 03/10/14

Today we went through Harecastle tunnel, it's a whooper at almost 2 miles long! It is single file only so it's manned both ends, they let a certain number of boats in one end and then they shut the doors both ends so they can suck out the fumes, daunting! They do let you out the other side though don't panic. Also, weirdly the tunnel has ironstone in it so the canal water both sides is bright orange, a similar shade to the chosen colour of the reality TV celebrity, oompa loompa.

As I imagined the tunnel was ridiculously dark, smelly, wet and absolutely freezing - I loved it, not sure what that says about me. We had the head light on at the front and a large hand held torch with us at the back. Roly driving, me holding the torch. Not very well apparently, well the fascinating stalactites on the ceiling and on the tunnel sides kept distracting me.

After doing more duplicate locks earlier today, I have discovered that if there are two of you going up you can have a race, mind you if they don't know about it you can hardly call it a race so I'll rephrase that, you can secretly try and beat them. It's like a Sat Nav, whenever I went anywhere that I needed directions for (most places to be fair) I had to beat the time It was like an obsession, if Tom tells me it would take an hour to get there I had to do it in less, surely everyone tries to beat the time on their Tom Tom?!

We did our first night driving today, I say we, I mean him. I got bored of the 'not here, just a little bit further' hours ago so was inside doing a jigsaw. He finally admitted defeat at 7:30, which in August would have been a lovely summers evening, but in October was pitch black. I heard 'Jayne I need a hand', I thought, no dear, you need night vision googles not a hand. Mooring up in the dark is no fun, but we got it done.

Travelling - Hem Heath - to - Stone
Date - 04/10/14

I saw an information box along the route today, it was near a lock so I hopped off to investigate. It needed the British Waterways key to open it, oh it must be a secret special thing for canal folk only, and inside, sadly no treasure but a bunch of leaflets advertising a food festival and farmers market in the next town. That's me loving Stone already!

We pitched up, excited and ready to buy a ridiculous amount of overpriced deli produce. I was in my element, lots of quirky unusual foodstuff, booze and a band. We will be eating olives, dried sausage and cheese for weeks. Roly found a cider that kept him happy, at 7.5% it also made him wobbly and a bit giggly, he is going to feel that tomorrow. He quite sincerely declared Stone the best place ever, and then started to dance along to the Irish band. I discovered battercakes. Pancake balls that you have a filling squished into the centre, Nutella and cherries in my case. What glorious sweet stodge, why is there not a battercakes stand on every corner and why at almost 40 have I never heard of them nor eaten them ever before.

Travelling - Stone - to - Nowhere
Date - 05/10/14

We aren't moving today, Roly isn't capable. Poor poor man is unwell. Tried to remind him of his cider fueled antics, but no, apparently it definitely isn't a hangover, he is very definitely ill, yes dear if you say so. I'll look after him, a fry up, snacks & an animated film should help with whatever 'virus' has struck.

Travelling - Stone - to - Nowhere
Date - 06/10/14

We are going nowhere today, the wind and rain dictate. Aside from emptying the toilet and popping to the supermarket we are just going to curl up on the sofa, Even Roly has sympathy for the holiday boaters forced to move on in this weather. Rain I like, I have no objection to getting a bit soggy, but I detest the wind and the two together are just nasty, so Stone has us for another day.

Whilst Roly emptied the loo, I thought I would use the facilities and came across the usual selection of books with a printed notice offering book exchange courtesy of the Canal & River Trust volunteers. Someone had written, as in, taken time out of their day to go and get a pen to write 'sorry but this (book exchange) has been around a lot longer than the volunteers, it's nice though thanks'. What the ......! I bet that was a woman, a man wouldn't notice, or if he did he wouldn't care enough to make the point. That is a passive aggressive woman with too much time on her hands, hang on that could be me! No, no this woman has clearly lived on the water for a long time. In fact she has probably staked out a claim on ownership of the water and will, no doubt have the same view on canal users with less than 20yrs hard toil as Roly does for hire boaters.

Travelling - Stone - to - Forwards
Date - 07/10/14

At about 12 today the heavens opened, why are we so surprised and disappointed when the weather turns. It's October, realistically we have done well, I have been in shorts for most of our trip (although these lily whites look like they have been hidden away for about 6 years not greeting the sun daily). We knew wet and cold was going to happen, so time to man up and deal with it. About half an hour later it dawned on me, why were we persisting in battling the elements, we had nowhere we needed to be. This pair of idiots wearing an assortment of waterproofs and brandishing a golfing umbrella could have been moored up relaxing in front of the fire, laughing at the poor idiots out in it. So that's what we did, better late than never.

Travelling - Towpath opposite a field of cows - to - Onwards
Date - 08/10/14

I never knew canal boats were such a work in progress. it seems everyday something needs fixing or tweaking, it is a good job Roly is so hands on, I'd have given up ages ago if he was as clueless as me. The water tank was obviously a biggie, but we have also had a leaky sink, broken door catches and a broken toilet handle. He has also fixed the shower pump (the button you press to make the water go away, whilst you are showering). Which stupid me didn't understand when we first got on board, assuming the water would just drain away like it does in the sinks, but no the shower tray is below the water level. Not only would the water not drain away, but more seriously the boat would fill with canal water and sink. 'Oh yeah' I exclaimed when Roly pointed out the flaw in having a hole under your boat for shower water to just drain out of, no don't laugh.

Today the oven grill has decided to sulk about something and is refusing to work unless you hold the temperature button in. I do think gas appliances should be outside of Roly's handyman remit, so do we call in an expert or do we ignore the grill from now on? Who needs a grill anyway? Except of course for the all-important cheese on toast. Decisions, decisions.

We had thunder, lightning and hail today, thankfully we managed to get to the pub before it started, unfortunately that did mean we had to stay for a few until it stopped. A little worse for wear on the walk back to the boat we tossed a coin to decide whether to move on or stay as the weather had cleared .
. . .

Wrong decision, 5 minutes after we set off, it started up again. Nothing for it but to carry on. Then, yes, of course there was a lock. As a chivalrous partner, Roly of course did the lock. Which as he was half cut he seemed to thoroughly enjoy. Bouncing around like a 7year in a kagool, whilst I wrestled the tiller and a big arsed umbrella.

Travelling - Weston on Trent - to - That way
Date - 09/10/14

We pulled up to a lock today where a boat towing a working boat was about to use the lock. Not seen this before, so we tied off and went for a gawk. First, they had to untie and moor up the tow-ee boat so they could take the tow-er boat down (single locks see, not double). Once down, they tied the tow-er boat to the lock gate, refilled the lock and set about getting the tow-ee boat in, as it had no engine they had to pull it in then also tie it to the lock gate. Just two men were doing this whole operation. One let the paddles up very slowly (so as not to un-nerve the tow-er boat literally sitting outside the lock), the other man held both ropes so he could loosen & tighten them as the water level changed, I imagine probably for dear life in respect of the tow-er boat being forced back by the water charging out of the lock. Once empty again, they quickly opened the gates, untied the ropes and scampered down to jump on each boat. The guy on the front boat reversed partly into the open lock up to the engineless boat and tied them back together. The guy in the second boat re-attached a tiller to the most enormous wooden rudder, so once they were off again he could help steer. Most fascinating and performed like a well-oiled machine. (We did offer to help, but they had a system they stuck too, just so you know we didn't literally just gawk like tourists)!

Even the man who lived in the house next to the lock came out for a look and a chat. Turns out he was born on the canal, as was his father, as was his father before him etc etc, of course. He had about 100 bits of advice for us often referring to nearside and offside, called Roly kid and me lass. He was most displeased to hear we had 'done' the Llangollen, I'm sure he referred to it as a tin bottom bath or something similar but to be honest I'd glazed over a bit by then. What did bring me back to the land of the concentrating was his absolute disgust at women doing the locks, whilst the men stayed on the boats, his words 'any idiot can steer a bloody boat but the locks are bloody hard work'. For a tiny second I was cruelly tempted to say, 'yes he makes me do all the locks and I have to carry coal and logs regularly too', whilst looking all fragile and girly, but the moment passed and I came to Roly's aid and reassured the man we took it in turns and that it was my choice to share. What I didn't admit, was that a lot of us 'new' canal ladies didn't like an audience whilst learning to navigate into a narrow lock, nor can we be arsed with the men folk moaning if we scrape their precious toys albeit in the same place they themselves did it two days ago and finally we are utterly convinced a few locks a day will banish the bingo wings forever.

Travelling - Rugeley- to - A bit further
Date - 10/10/14

Today I've seen 2 geese and 1 swan all with a few feathers stripped off their wings, leaving just quills sticking out. What's that all about, a water bird fight club perhaps or is someone trying to re stuff a pillow?

I have also noticed a lot of private moorings with a caravan on their 'patch'. So they have a boat and a caravan, I suppose it's no different to having an actual house and a caravan. Except the obvious, the boat moves, use that! It just seems odd to me, maybe the caravan is the proverbial dog house, boats aren't a very big space for a tiff.

Travelling - Armitage- to - Onwards
Date - 11/10/14

Around these parts the locks come with bridges, I don't mean the lock is next to a road or a pedestrian bridge, although they often are. I mean the lock has a little bridge across it so that you don't have to make any death defying leaps to get across or run (walk) back to the other end to cross over the closed lock gates if it's too wide or slippery on the already open side. The bridge makes life a little easier, bit like a T.V remote. But why, oh why do they need to put the bridges so close to the gates, so that when you have opened said gate you have to clamber over the huge wooden apparatus to then use the bridge. Honestly, I look ridiculous shimmying up and over with my short legs, I think you need to be a long limbed athlete or a catwalk model to step over those things gracefully, or a giraffe of course.

Saw something funny this afternoon. It was hilarious, well until it wasn't funny anymore. We pulled up behind a hire boat waiting to go down the lock, I knew it was going to be fun to watch as they had approached the towpath head on or bow first to use the boating term (ohh get me). You need to sort of pull alongside it, bit like parking a car on the kerbside . He leapt off to pull in the rest of the boat, once settled and adjacent to the towpath the missus climbed down to take hold of the centre rope, leaving husband free to get back on board or in this case, fall in. Yes, my first overboard incident witnessed and surprisingly it wasn't Roly or myself. After checking he resurfaced and was breathing, I allowed myself a small chuckle, or two. Wifey on the other hand went into mild panic mode as his water aerobics had frightened the boat so much it was trying to escape her clutches, so much so that a passing cyclist leapt off his bike to rush to her aid. We pulled up behind them just as the boat ahead of them pulled off to enter the lock and so began the fiasco of soggy man and jittery woman trying to get their boat out of the weeds to move up to the mooring posts now a space had been freed up. By the time they had managed it, I was really struggling, it felt like I was watching a comedy sketch that I absolutely was not allowed to laugh at. Mission accomplished, phew they made it. I strolled past them swinging my windlass looking everywhere but there at her sobbing and him dripping. I still felt the whole thing was funny and no 'laughing at other peoples misfortune' guilt had set in yet as I proceeded to help the next boat come up. It wasn't until she wandered over to help out that I started to feel bad. The poor woman was traumatised, she was shaking like a leaf, anybody that hadn't witnessed the ridiculous episode could have mistaken her for a surviving victim of a tornado. I did the right thing and asked if they were ok and suggested perhaps hubby got changed, we were in no rush and were happy to wait, but no this woman was on a mission to get past this ghastly place so they could stop for a cup of tea. Tea! She needed a large vodka and a valium in my opinion. In the drama, she had hurt her hand. It was bruised and bleeding, so yes I then felt even worse for sniggering earlier. In a quivery voice, she declared she hated it and would never get on a canal boat again. I tried to reassure her it would get easier, but I suspect this perhaps hadn't been their first incident and that when she returned the hire boat on Wednesday (only Saturday today), she would kiss the ground and never look back.

Travelling - Fradley Junction - to - Coventry way
Date - 12/10/14

It's all about leaves today, obviously leaves have featured greatly already as it is autumn but today is especially windy. They are dominating the sky and are swirling in the water.

Leaves are, much to Roly's surprised annoyance taking up residence on top of the boat, I'm not sure where he thought they would choose to lay for their final decay if we opted to moor up under the trees that have shed them, but brushing the roof whilst chuntering about it is a new morning routine.

Where are all the stunning colours that the UK saw last year, is it still a bit warm? So far we have just green (still attached) or brown, with an occasional yellow thrown in. I was hoping for reds and oranges at the very least. Thus far, I haven't photographed one interesting bush or tree. A relief, no doubt for the poor people subjected to my album when I get home, but disappointing for me.

Travelling - No idea - to - Straight on
Date - 14/10/14

We are map-less and have been since Fradley Junction two days ago. Our collection of canal maps doesn't include the one we are on now. It's not a worry, we are hardly going to get lost on a canal, they are just handy for letting you know where things are, water point, toilet emptying and of course the pubs. Pearson map companions show everything and I highly recommend them if you decide to hit the water.

We have tried to obtain a map book several times but South Midlands section is proving to be elusive. The first chandlers (that's a boat shop to you and I) was closed, the second had every map book but South Midlands, including a large selection of full priced earlier editions, surely anyone purchasing a canal map would want the most up to date editions. Maybe there are collectors out there, people that have converted their spare rooms to pay homage to Pearsons maps, or indeed any maps. The third chandlers didn't stock Pearsons at all, so currently we are being super hard core and going it alone. Where has the control freak in me gone?

Saw 3 female pheasants earlier. They were walking in procession, and then one by one they hopped through a gap in the hedgerow. Why were they walking single file together, had they dropped the kids off at school and were off to get coffee. Had they recently discovered they were dating the same male pheasant and were heading his way to have it out, who knows!

Travelling - Tamworth - to – That-a-way
Date - 15/10/14

Still no map book but as we stopped to do a shop we know we are in Tamworth. We went to a supermarket to get the essentials, you know wine and vegetables, water and chocolate. The supermarket had two storeys, two whole floors of supermarket stuff, that is just too much. It was crazy big. Maybe I'm just getting old but do we really need 750 varieties of crisps, 400 different types of bread and thousands of different biscuits? I wish we could rein it in a bit, well a lot actually.

I was disturbed to see an injured mallard earlier, some well-rounded individual had shot this duck with a little crossbow arrow. I'm sure the duck didn't imagine for one second that eating bread and quacking was cause for attempted murder. I'd very much like that pillar of community to be shot in the arm, (for it was the ducks wing that was displaying the brightly coloured weapon) and not with his mini crossbow either, a big arsed one like Daryl uses in The Walking Dead, then we leave that arrow sticking out of his arm until a kindly duck comes along to remove it. We pulled over to try and help said duck, but half a loaf of bread and 1 failed attempt at covering him with Roly's jacket and we had to stop. The poor thing didn't need Laurel and Hardy making his life any more difficult, we called the RSPCA instead, assume they at least have a net and some skills.

Travelling - Past Tamworth - to - South
Date - 16/10/14

There aren't many boats on the cut now, when I mentioned that to Roly he pointed out its October not August, good point only idiots that live on boats like us will be about soon. Although they haven't all finished just yet. We watched a hire boat of middle-aged men get stuck earlier, hugely entertaining. Us and them met at a water point, as you do. They left first, all hopping aboard after exchanging lots of banter. They untied and pushed off and strangely, that then seemed to be it. I have no idea what happened next, maybe everyone thought someone else was steering, or maybe they just thought they would let the boat decide where it wanted to go. Anyhow, when I next looked up, crew and boat were stuck fast in the weeds opposite. They had literally just pushed off one side of the canal to get stuck on the other side. Now, this group of 5 men didn't have a captain, instead they had 5. The whole quintet began barking instructions at each other, whilst Roly & I admired from afar. Someone grabbed the throttle and put her in hard forward, two had grabbed the barge pole and were pushing with all their might backwards and two were on the roof sword fighting. No, that last one was a lie, they were just laughing hysterically. They got free in the end, luck rather than judgement by the looks of it and sadly they were going in the opposite direction to us so I couldn't follow their antics further.

I am absolutely convinced I just saw Father Christmas at a set of locks we passed through, he was volunteering as the lock keeper. It's far too late in the year for him to be helping out at locks, he must have tons to do in the North Pole surely. Of course it could have been Captain Birdseye, I can never tell those two apart when they aren't wearing their uniforms.

Travelling - Near Nuneaton- to - Past Nuneaton
Date - 17/10/14

Finally purchased a map today, thank-you Springwood Haven for being fully stocked in Pearsons Canal Companions. The novelty of being without a map was starting to wear off. We kept trying to stop for lunch yesterday but met a lock at every turn. 13 locks later and we finally ate at 3.30pm. So now we again know what is around the next bend we can plan a bit beforehand.

Yet another handyman job for Roly this morning before we set off. Is it just our boat or are they all a work in progress? For a few weeks the water has run down to nothing whilst the tap is on, a mild inconvenience, as after a few seconds it starts to run again and all is well, , , Then it got worse, a few more seconds wait. . . . Then this morning a lot longer, not a problem if you're washing up but bloody nasty when you are showering. Never has a shower cubicle heard such profanities as mine as when I was soapy, dripping and ever so slightly bloody freezing, stood waiting for the water to return to the party. Roly was presented with an ultimatum, either fix it or face heavy financial losses as I rake up the tab at every hotel along the way. That got him replacing the water pump sharpish.

Travelling - Past Bedworth - to - Onwards
Date - 18/10/14

I saw a sign from the Canal and River Trust earlier, it was a warning and had a red background as in Danger - notice this. It warned us to stay 2 metres away from the offside due to obstructions for 100 metres. That's when Roly & I realised we didn't know which side was 'off' on the boat. I know it's driver side in a car, the steering wheel is furthest from the kerb. In a boat the steering is centre. Obviously, we stuck to the middle, closed our eyes and hoped for the best. That strategy worked, I may use it again.

Saw another sign, this one so wonderful I insisted we moor up for the rest of the day. A pub on the side of the canal had a sandwich board advertising the usual, dogs welcome, kids welcome, lovely ales and lovelier food etc and nestled in amongst the 'you know you want to pay us a visit sales pitch' were the words bathroom hire. I practically leapt off the boat before we had stopped, literally charged into the pub and practically knocked Saturday drinkers flying to get to the bar. Once there, for some reason, I became an idiot, "Hi, can I hire a bath here?" "yes" "as in a bath with bubbles" "yes, we hire out bathrooms" "as in I can have an actual bath here", at this point I think he was trying to edge away from me, so to make sure he knew I wasn't crazy I reassured him with "sorry, I'm just excited about possibly having a bath", that helped I'm sure. Then I got worried he may think I was homeless so said "I have a shower on the boat I live on, I just miss a bath". Jeez shut up Jayne before they close the pub on your scary arse! Turns out it was £10.00 to hire the bathroom, well you got the whole hotel room, so I booked it obviously. Nice as the room was, it didn't interest me, I only had eyes for the bath. Best £10 I have spent on this trip so far. The Barley Mow in Newbold I salute you. 2

hours, half a bottle of wine and a good chunk of my book, perfect.

Travelling - Newbold - to - Somewhere else
Date - 19/10/14

I was inside the boat washing earlier, minding my own and getting on with chores when there was this almighty bang and everything on the boat shot forward several inches, me included! I popped my head out of the side door looking for icebergs or a giant meteor, to see only a very pale looking Roly saying 'I didn't see it'. I retreated back into the boat having established he was still on board and started picking up our scattered possessions, closing every door on the boat and tried to calm my racing heart before it leapt to safety canalside, unbelievably nothing broke. Turns out Roly had moved over a bit as a boat was approaching and he hadn't spotted a narrowing of the canal, a large area of stone jutting out. To say we crapped ourselves would be an understatement so we pulled over to calm our nerves and to see how quickly she would sink, for I was expecting a gaping hole or at least a suitably impressive dent, turns out these boats are made of stern stuff we only had a scratch to show for it. And when he wasn't looking I threw my hands in the air & whispered 'thank feck I didn't do it'.

Travelling - Norton Junction - to - Nether Heyford
Date - 22/10/14

Instead of taking the Oxford turning at Braunston junction we took the Grand Union, heading home way.

We had many family and friend visits in the last few days (hence why I've been silent on the writing front) and more visits to come in the next couple of days. It was really nice to catch up and I got to dump a load of washing on my sister. Heading to The Narrow Boat pub to meet up with the Aunt and Uncle later, can't wait. We have missed so many people on our trip, even with all our regular visitors so it's nice to cram so much in.

I did the driving at the locks today and as they were double locks we shared with another boat. I did fine, no idea what I was so worried about. I didn't sink either boat, fall in, crash or perform any other boating faux pas. As far as I'm concerned I am now an expert, I can do this canaling lark.

Travelling - Weedon - to - Gayton
Date - 23/10/14

Passed The Wharf at Bugbrooke today, that was where we started our journey from 3 months ago. It made me think just how much I've changed in that short time. I've not put any makeup on, I've not had to have order in my day, I've not ironed anything I've washed let alone EVERYTHING I've washed, in my previous life I was a little bit addicted to ironing. Turns out, as a boat gypsy I don't need perfect straights. My poor sister, bless her, didn't know about my transformation. She took my bag of washing, jeans, towels & bedding because they, without doubt, are my very least favorite things to hand wash and because she knows me so well, excuse me, knew me so well she ironed the lot. Perhaps I should have told her!

Travelling - Gayton - to - Stoke Bruene
Date - 24/10/14

Today is our 3 month anniversary, I should be celebrating by washing my hair. I decided when we came on this trip I would try that experiment where you don't shampoo your hair for 3 months and taa-daa after that period it miraculously self-cleans. Unsurprisingly, that didn't work, although I admitted defeat and gave up a week short of the end date. For 3 months, I have been living in headscarves and hats, furiously scrubbing my scalp and hair with just shower water. It never got any greasier than greasy and unbelievably some days it looked ok, it felt thick (undoubtedly a lard build up) which made a nice change my usual baby fine hair. The decider in quitting was Roly casually telling me my hair smelt musty. That was it game over, I am not having that! 3 shampoos later and I had squeaky clean, apple scented flyaway hair. Oh well it was worth a try.

We did Blisworth tunnel today, 3076 yards, over 1.5miles in a pitch black tunnel, with just a headlight 57 feet ahead of you and a large hand torch at the back that I'm in charge of and sometimes accidentally move up the walls to look for interesting growths. Bit nerve wrecking in this one as we had passed a boat coming the other way. It was a tight squeeze and Roly got a bit tense, so I helped by waving the torch at the ceiling and making wooo ghost noises. What would he do without my helpfulness.

Travelling - Stoke Bruene - to - Nowhere
Date - 25/10/14

Had some friends over today. Went up the canal a bit then turned around and came back, just so everyone got a go at driving and doing the locks, kids loved it and we enjoy showing her off.

Crossed something off my bucket list today, not a usual addition to a wish list and perhaps an everyday occurrence for country folk but today I got to stroke a cow for the first time. Walking back to the boat and some cows had wandered from their field into a wooded area, both field and woods were fenced off from the towpath but one cow clearly had ambitions to check out what she may have been missing and was standing very close to the fence. So I approached slowly, so as not to come on to strong and she didn't object or run for it. Then I was right there, close enough to touch her head if she let me and she did. Must have been my clean hair, or I'm completely over thinking it and I am not a cow whisperer, it's just this cow loves people and regularly get a head rub.

We shared locks today with a hire boat, hugely entertaining as every time and I honestly mean every single time that they grabbed their centre rope they knocked something into the water. We laughed along with them, oh ha ha there goes our barge pole, oh titter there goes our bucket. The poor man driving spent quite a lot of his time running, well cautiously walking down the side of their boat collecting items out of the water. Wonder if they ever learnt or spent the rest of their boating holiday dunking random objects.

Travelling - Stoke Bruene - to - Still here
Date - 26/10/14

Another busy day of visitors today, more friends came over so that meant another round trip, people are going to think us strange just going up & down the same strip of water. This time however I'm not convinced everyone was sober. I blame the Talletts, fancy arranging to meet in a pub, everyone knows when Franky and I get together a vast amount of wine is usually involved. Actually as we made it onto the boat and did indeed leave the pub I think we did well there.

The Parkers came later and that again meant another pub visit, damn this entertaining guests is hard work. Didn't move the boat with these folk, not because we didn't trust them not to fall in, more likely we were bored of that same stretch of canal and unable to manage the task anyway.

Then to close the evening, a curry with the offspring, which of course meant yet more wine, my liver may demand some respite soon. Still mustn't grumble, wine, friends and family, I can live with that on a Sunday, the liver will just have to manage.

Travelling - Stoke Bruene - to - Somewhere else
Date - 27/10/14

We are on our way again today. Visits are over so heading off to pastures new. It won't be far, as we are near home and some decisions need to be made about where to next. Glad to see the back of those locks though we had done them so many times.

As punishment for laughing at the misfortune of the last hire boat we shared the locks with, karma has delivered us another hire boat to share with. A quartet of the more mature variety had only collected their hire boat yesterday so were a bit cautious to say the least. Each time we got to a lock they used all three ropes to tie up with front, centre and rear. I know canal life is handled at a leisurely pace, but I did get a little feeling inside, like you do when rushing around on your lunch break and get stuck behind the old biddy with her trolley on wheels, having the most relaxing day of her life and wanting to share her life story with anyone close enough to listen. I know,

I know that will be me one day. I remember thinking when I was younger, much much younger, bloody hell when I get old I shall not go near any shops during lunch breaks, I'll go at different times because I will be in the way. Now I know I shall more than likely be thinking I'll do as I please thank you, so you stand there with your boots sandwich whilst I recount my great grandsons role in the school nativity to the shop assistant. Anyway I digress, I had a word with myself, slapped that smile on & tackled those locks slowly, not like I had to get back to the office anytime soon.

Travelling - Cosgrove - to - Who knows
Date - 28/10/14

I just drove into a lock in my slippers. It'll be in my PJ's next you wait. All Roly's fault of course, I was inside the boat, washing some smalls when we pulled up at a lock. He didn't give me a warning or anything, suddenly we were just there and ready to go. I thought sod it, I'll just do it, no one will notice and then of course, along came a grandad and 2 kids to watch and help, then another boat appeared so I was caught like a deer in headlights and ended up lock sharing with an audience in my slippers. So conscious of being in my slippers I was, that I failed to notice or remember I was actually bra-less too. The look on my face as the penny dropped a few miles later had Roly hanging onto the boat edge in stiches, I will most definitely get him back.

Saw hundreds of Canadian geese at Cosgrove, It looked like that every single one in the world had all travelled there, why? What is so special about Cosgrove, had they all agreed to meet up or something whilst migrating. 'Hey fancy stopping at Cosgrove, they do a fantastic lunch in the field there', 'yeah why not, I'll let the boys know'.

I saw a man showing his dog a plane, a plane in the actual sky. We were travelling along the canal so sadly I couldn't hear the exchange between man and dog, but he stopped, bent down to talk to the dog and then pointed up at a plane in the sky. Unsurprisingly the dog didn't raise his paw and wave, he didn't even lift his head in acknowledgement, so I'm not sure of the point but then I'm not a dog person, perhaps that's a common occurrence on walks. Nowt as queer as folk as they say.

Travelling - Milton Keynes - to - South
Date - 29/10/14

We followed a boat with an L plate on the side and a young lad at the tiller earlier, I thought that was considerate. He drove very well, just really really slowly, we weren't even in drive some of time, just coasting. At least with the plates, we knew & just were happy to slowly bob along. Good excuse to slow down the pace of life another notch, don't want to get to crazy wild out here.

Saw another first today. A cruiser, they look like baby yachts, moored up at its own long term mooring site with a tent pitched up on the land. I thought the boat/caravan combo was weird, but baby boat and 1 man tent is even odder in my non-imaginative mind. Neither of those 'homes' give you room to raise your arms, let along stretch. I'd take cabin fever to a whole new level if I had to live in those two.

Travelling - Simpson - to - That way a bit
Date - 30/10/14

We moored up using pins yesterday, they are a bit like giant tent pegs. In the early afternoon the boat started to bang a bit when other boats passed, not in protest that we had restrained her honest, just because, we assumed, a rope was working loose. As it was chucking it down and we were mid-way through a film we left it to tighten later. Then a boat came passed at speed, I use the term speed loosely, but no slowing down occurred and again we banged against the canalside. I glanced up, out of the porthole and thought that view looks unusual, did a double take and yes, the boat was definitely up to something odd. The front of Billow was making its way lazily across the canal ready to meet the other side, whilst the back was still snug and secure against the bank we had tied her too. Turns out our pin had snapped, how did that even happen? Those things are thick steel. In the pouring rain we had to scrabble around trying to pull the front back in whilst laughing like hyenas.

We did Fenny lock today. A whole one foot, 1 inch 'tall' and across the lock was a road bridge. I don't mean a bridge the boaters pass under I mean an actual bit of road you have to swing out of the way. I do 'get' both. Ok there is a tiny difference in canal height, so we need a lock to go up or down and again I understand a road needs to happen for convenience and quicker access to those newish houses and a swing bridge is likely to have been the cheapest option, but together, a lock and a swing bridge is an awful lot of work for a mere foot of water.

Travelling - Stoke Hammond - to - Who knows
Date - 31/10/14

Happy Halloween, I don't even have a pumpkin. I do however, have a bag of fun size Mars Bars, which Roly has been banned from eating, just in case boat folk trick or treat.

Soulbury locks, what a farce we had doing those today. I am not sure the volunteer on today could have organised a piss up in a brewery. In the mix, when we arrived was a wide beam being towed by a standard width, then two narrow boats tied side by side, thus creating another double width and then a hire boat, all these were coming down the thee lock tier. We were going up. Granted that combination was most unusual but the volunteer asked the towing team to separate so that we could start ascending from the bottom staircase, then he asked the hire boat to wait in the middle basin, so as to bring down the conjoined twins. When we got to the middle lock there were 3 boats also there, halfway down. He asked me to wait in the lock and got the twins to leave their lock to pull into the left, where the hire boat was already pulled into. That was no mean feat, these boats are not made for moving well in tight spaces and the pools between staircase locks are small, so doing it with two boats together certainly took a while. Thankfully, we shook off the helpful volunteer for the third and final lock as he was still trying to negotiate the convoy of odd boats down. Just when we thought we were away free, a cygnet snuck into the lock as I was driving out. Couldn't bear to leave it trapped between two shut gates so Roly had to try and coax it out with bread and encouraging words. Not sure how much his talking helped, probably about as much as my uncontrollable laughter.

Travelling - Leighton - to - Back a bit
Date - 01/11/14

It rained last night, clearly not the first time we have experienced British weather on our British trip, but at 5 O'clock this morning I thought the entire cast of River Dance had climbed aboard to practice on our roof. I woke with a start, heart in my mouth type thing, convinced we were being fired upon. The rain on the roof is usually quite a nice relaxing sound, no that was definitely not the case this morning.

Travelling - Old Linslade - to - Stoke Hammond & back again
Date - 02/11/14

More visitors today. Wendy and Andy, my Aunt and Uncle came for a day trip, Roly even shared the driving with them, he's a bit possessive of his baby. I think one of us had to prise his fingers off the tiller (need to note that worry may have come from me, a friend and her associated children all doing it at once and crashing into some overhanging bushes a while ago, ohh we did get told off) .

We lock shared with a lady that was telling Wendy and I a tale about somcone leaving their weed hatch open and the boat sinking. We are both doing all the smiling and nodding in the right places, it wasn't until after we parted company Wendy asked what a wee hole was, I may have sniggered a little.

Travelling - Leighton Buzzard - to - Onwards
Date - 03/11/14

No idea what lives in this stretch of the Gran Union, but whatever they are there are lots of them and they create lots and lots of bubbles. Roly say they are fish, but why so bubbly on this bit of the canal, I've never seen so much. The water looks like a murky Aero.

I helped an elderly man carry his shopping across the lock today, it was heavy and he looked a bit wobbly. As I hopped up onto the lock with his groceries, he said 'I've got lung cancer you know'. Where am I supposed to go with that little conversation starter?! Oh that's a shame, doesn't really cover it. Thankfully, he moved onto other subjects swiftly.

In the next lock were two cygnets. That is just rude, someone has come down the lock, let themselves out but left the birds in there. Both were trying frantically to get out but they were unable to fly out of the lock, as they need a bigger runway. No idea how long they had been stuck in there. When we opened the gate they were off like a shot, I hope they found mum and dad as they seemed quite young.

Travelling - Near Ivinghoe - to - That way
Date - 04/11/14

Not many boats on the move now. The two we saw before lunch were live aboard men on their own. The first was an unusual combination of man, skinhead with tattoos on his scalp and face and a bright orange goatee, but very very well spoken (exchanged pleasantries at a lock). Not often those two ends of the spectrum meet in a single person. Desperately wanted his back story, I bet it was interesting, but figured it would be rude to start grilling a complete stranger as we went through a lock. The second guy was just as uninteresting as Roly & I so he won't get a mention.

What is it with all the spider silk floating about today. There are thousands of strands swaying about in the breeze. They may look beautiful shimmering in the sunlight, but they mean only one thing, spiders. Disgusting creatures with their weird legs, creepy walk and plots to assassinate me. I think I would cope better if they had less eyes as scorpions don't give me the heebie geebies and they have 8 legs, although saying that, pretty sure I would lose my shit if a scorpion just randomly darted out from under the sofa.

Travelling - Heading back again
Date - 05/11/14

Had a scary experience today. I drove into a double lock earlier and because ours was the only boat in there she drifted a bit when the gates closed and I ended up at an angle with the front end pointing a little north west, the rear, a little south east across the water. Roly then lifted the first paddle to let water out and something weird happened. I didn't notice it at first, but as he was climbing over the lock gates to get to the other paddle I felt a lean to the right. It was too early for wine, even for me, so why was I slowly tipping to the right? Took a moment or two to work out if I had suddenly developed vertigo, but no, Billow and I were definitely listing to the right. I then asked Roly to close the paddle, well actually I screamed at him 'quick shut the thingy somethings wrong'. As he darted back he spotted that the gunnel (the sticky out lip bit running down the side) had caught on the edge of the concrete lock wall. So as the water was rushing out our front was staying hooked up on the edge. In all likelihood the boat would have slipped off as the water level decreased because it only took a hard shove from Roly's foot to push her back into the water, but in that moment of panic I visualised Billow tipping over and squashing me on the bottom, not my bottom obviously, the bottom of the lock chamber.

Travelling - Stoke Hammond - to - Home
Date - 06/11/14

We pulled over as the rain started and as I was at the sink filling the kettle I spotted a kingfisher, he was perched on the tiller of another boat moored up on the opposite side of the canal. We daren't open the side door to take a picture as no doubt he would fly away so we pulled the glass out of the porthole, that isn't as drastic as it sounds, they all come out with a slight lift up and back. I now finally have a picture of a kingfisher, maybe he knew that was the one thing I was disappointed to have not got on this trip. Like a kid collecting Panini stickers I have heaps of duck and heron pictures, just struggled to get one of the allusive Kingfisher. My sticker book is now complete.

Decided to head home tomorrow. As in terra firma, my brick built non floating house. Our journey is done and as they say in Game of Thrones, winter is coming.

What an amazing experience we have had and I'm glad to have done something outside of the normal 9-5. I wonder how long it will take me to revert back to my 'normal' way of life. I know I can't live on a boat permanently, it's not for me, but a 3ish month break from the world, yes, it turns out that I can do. Will miss so much of what has become our daily life but boy I cannot wait for a bath, a washing machine and a bed big enough to starfish in at my daily disposal.

The End

30238049R00060

Printed in Poland
by Amazon Fulfillment
Poland Sp. z o.o., Wrocław